# Praise for *Finally Free*

**Finally Free** is not the typical man-ce...
reader shallow teachings and a hope...
systematically builds his case fo...
solutions provided by God's Word. Fr...
chapter, he persistently points the re...
Deliverer and Solution. I hi...

Steve Gallagher, founder of Pure Life Ministries
and author of *At the Altar of Sexual Idolatry*

Heath Lambert writes from his heart of love for God and love for others.
The Scriptures he includes are alive and powerful. His applications
are insightful and practical. **Finally Free** is exceptionally well written
and clear. I highly recommend this book to anyone struggling with
pornography. There is truly hope, grace, and mercy to be finally free.

Martha Peace, biblical counselor
and author of *The Excellent Wife*

Finally, a book to help people struggling with pornography that isn't
focused on pornography! What we need is forgiving, empowering, and
transforming grace, which Heath Lambert invites strugglers to experience
by embracing Christ and following him in these grace-empowered
biblical strategies.

Mike Wilkerson, director of biblical counseling
at Mars Hill Church, Seattle, Washington

Heath Lambert has biblically and practically addressed two devastating
problems: pornography and our ineffective response to it within the
church. His wise counsel is biblical because it begins and ends with God's
grace, and it is practical because it provides clear direction on how to
receive and grow in that grace. **Finally Free** is not just for individuals
struggling with porn; it is for everyone seeking to
follow Jesus and lead others to him in the twenty-first century.

Noel Bouché, president of Pure Hope Ministries

**Finally Free** offers gospel wisdom that will rush over the sin of lust like a mighty wave. Easy to read, presented in a winsome pastoral spirit, it balances grace and effort with expert precision. The theological message presented in these pages will not only overcome even the strongest pornography addiction; it will also seep into our entire spiritual life, renewing and invigorating us, turning victims into conquerors and captives into liberators.

Owen Strachan, executive director of the
Council on Biblical Manhood and Womanhood

I've read just about every Christian book on the topic of pornography. **Finally Free** is now the number-one book I'll recommend to pastors, counselors, strugglers, and those who love them.

Bob Kellemen, PhD, executive director of the Biblical Counseling Coalition
and author of *Sexual Abuse: Beauty for Ashes*

Countless people have fallen prey to the easy access of online pornography—even Christians. Heath Lambert speaks a prophetic word into this crisis and offers a gospel way out of addiction to pornography. I cannot think of a more timely or relevant book. It is for anyone who wants to know how to be **finally free** from this pervasive and deadly sin.

Denny Burk, associate professor of biblical studies at Boyce College

More than an exposé of the insidious power of pornography, **Finally Free** is a declaration of the amazing grace that frees us from this power. Heath Lambert offers a biblical, practical guide to the process God uses to bring about this freedom in our lives, all the while reminding us that grace is at the center of every strategy in the process.

Daniel Montgomery, founder and lead pastor of
Sojourn Community Church, Louisville, Kentucky

**Finally Free** provides biblical and wise discussions that offer specific, practical steps toward liberation from the clutches of pornography. Ultimately, the gospel of Jesus Christ is what sets us free here, as it does in every area, and Health Lambert lays out the joyous pathway to experience the gospel's true and lasting freedom.

Bruce Ware, professor of Christian theology,
The Southern Baptist Theological Seminary

# FINALLY
# FREE

# FINALLY
# FREE

## FIGHTING FOR PURITY
## WITH THE POWER OF GRACE

## HEATH LAMBERT

ZONDERVAN
REFLECTIVE

ZONDERVAN REFLECTIVE

*Finally Free*
Copyright © 2013 by Heath B. Lambert

Published in Grand Rapids, Michigan, by Zondervan. Zondervan is a registered trademark of The Zondervan Corporation, L.L.C., a wholly owned subsidiary of HarperCollins Christian Publishing, Inc.

Requests for information should be addressed to customercare@harpercollins .com.

Zondervan titles may be purchased in bulk for educational, business, fundraising, or sales promotional use. For information, please email SpecialMarkets@ Zondervan.com.

ISBN 978-0-310-49924-4 (ebook)

Library of Congress Cataloging-in-Publication Data

Lambert, Heath, 1979-
    Finally free : fighting for purity with the power of grace / Heath Lambert.
        p. cm.
    ISBN 978-0-310-49923-7 (pbk.)
    1. Pornography—Religious aspects—Christianity. 2. Liberty—Religious—Christianity. 3. Grace (Theology). I. Title.
BV4597.6.L36 2013
241'.667—dc23
2012048818

*Cover design: Brand Navigation*
*Cover photography: GettyImages, iStockphoto*
*Interior design: Ben Fetterley; Greg Johnson/Textbook Perfect*

*Printed in the United States of America*

24 25 26 27 28  LBC  61 60 59 58 57

To my beloved and precious sons,
Carson and Connor.

A wicked world seeks to enslave your souls to pornography;
the grace of Jesus Christ alone sets you free.

Look to him!

# Contents

INTRODUCTION The Purpose of This Book . . . . . . . . . . . . . . . . . . . . . . 11

CHAPTER 1 Grace as the Foundation in the Fight
Against Pornography . . . . . . . . . . . . . . . . . . . . . . . . . 17

CHAPTER 2 Using Sorrow to Fight Pornography . . . . . . . . . . . . 31

CHAPTER 3 Using Accountability to Fight Pornography . . . . . . 45

CHAPTER 4 Using Radical Measures to Fight Pornography . . . 59

CHAPTER 5 Using Confession to Fight Pornography . . . . . . . . . 75

CHAPTER 6 Using Your Spouse (or Your Singleness)
to Fight Pornography . . . . . . . . . . . . . . . . . . . . . . . . 89

CHAPTER 7 Using Humility to Fight Pornography . . . . . . . . . . . 107

CHAPTER 8 Using Gratitude to Fight Pornography . . . . . . . . . . 121

CHAPTER 9 Using a Dynamic Relationship with Jesus
to Fight Pornography . . . . . . . . . . . . . . . . . . . . . . . . 135

CONCLUSION A Call to Holiness and Hope . . . . . . . . . . . . . . . . . . . 151

APPENDIX Help for Families and Friends of
Men Struggling with Pornography . . . . . . . . . . . . . 161

Acknowledgments . . . . . . . . . . . . . . . . . . . . . . . . . . . . . . . . . . . . . . . . . . 175

# INTRODUCTION:
# The Purpose of This Book

This book is not about pornography. You can find countless books *about* pornography. They include detailed information about the pornography industry—how many movies are made, what kinds of movies are made, how many people are involved, how much money is spent, and how many Internet sites are devoted to it. In this book, you will not find any information about the pornography industry.

Other books *about* pornography include long discussions about the damage pornography does—the layers of damage done to actors, the moral erosion within societies that embrace it, the physical and spiritual harm done to viewers, the carnage inflicted on marriages, the pain that afflicts the children and parents of consumers, and the incredible difficulty of defeating its temptations. This book is not about the catastrophic effects of pornography.

Other books *about* pornography spend a lot of time telling people how to think about pornography—how it is bad, how it stands in opposition to the kingdom of Jesus, how it goes against committed marital love, how it impedes ministry productivity, and how it harms one's Christian witness. It is not the purpose of this book to rewire your brain when it comes to pornography.

The goals of these other books are noble. There is a time and place to talk about all of these issues. But this book has a different purpose. For the past decade, I have spent thousands of hours talking with hundreds of people who struggle with pornography. I have never met anyone who experienced profound change because someone told them how many billions of dollars are spent on pornography every year. I have never met anyone whose life was radically changed by hearing (again) how damaging the pornography industry is and how they desperately need to think differently about it. Rather, every person I have ever talked to who sincerely wanted help already knew most of this information. People who are trapped in the deceitful web of pornography do not need more information *about* pornography.

This book is about something much better than pornography. This book is about the amazing power of Jesus Christ to free you from pornography.

In this book, I want to share with you the amazing depth and effect of Christ's power to eradicate pornography from your life. Whether you struggle with pornography yourself or are trying to help someone who struggles, I have good news for you: no matter how intense or long-standing the struggle, it is the work of Jesus Christ to set people free from such sin. Listen to the words of the apostle Paul:

> Do you not know that wrongdoers will not inherit the kingdom of God? Do not be deceived: *Neither the sexually immoral* nor idolaters nor adulterers nor men who have sex with men nor thieves nor the greedy nor drunkards nor slanderers nor swindlers *will inherit the kingdom of God. And that is what some of you were. But you were washed, you were sanctified, you were justified in the name of the Lord Jesus Christ and by the Spirit of our God.*

1 Corinthians 6:9–11, *emphasis added*

Do you see the power available to those who trust in Christ? Paul moves from condemnation to confidence. First, sin is powerfully condemned. The words are clear: if you are sexually immoral you will not inherit the kingdom of God. All those who look at pornography have only a fearful expectation of condemnation. Thankfully, Paul does not end there. He moves toward confidence in our Redeemer, Jesus. Jesus cleanses sinners. Jesus loves to cleanse those who love to look at pornography, and he loves to give them power to change. Our sinfulness does not get the final word. Instead, Jesus justifies, washes, and sanctifies us. Our only hope is in a risen Savior who has the power to bring us out of the pit of pornography. This book is a guide to the exciting process Jesus uses to do this work.

Jesus' power is extremely practical, and so this book is practical as well. Jesus will set you free from your struggle, but he also calls you to participate in his work. Again Paul writes, "Therefore, my dear friends, as you have always obeyed—not only in my presence, but now much more in my absence—continue to work out your salvation with fear and trembling, for it is God who works in you to will and to act in order to fulfill his good purpose" (Philippians 2:12–13).

God works in us so that we desire him and work for his good purpose. As Christians, we are able to do the work of obedience, but all of our growth is empowered by God's grace. Jesus gives us power to obey so that we can obey to the glory of God. Believers are called to lean on his strength, lay hold of practical means of grace, and take practical steps toward change.

For many years, I have counseled people who feel locked in a losing struggle against pornography. They need grace-filled, practically relevant strategies as they seek to flee sexual immorality. This book provides eight clear strategies to help you work out your salvation and experience freedom from your desire for pornography. These strategies are tools designed to help you turn from sin to righteousness based on the work of Christ. I have seen them work time and again. I pray you will see them work in your life and in the lives of those God has given you to help.

I hope you find this book practical and saturated with grace, but I also hope you find it to be pure. I have talked with more pastors, parents, and parishioners than I can count who are disappointed in the books available on pornography. They are disappointed because many of the resources they turn to for help are full of shocking—sometimes even vulgar—language. The resource they turned to for help often provided further temptations for the struggle they were trying to flee. I understand that. So does Paul: "Among you there must not be even a hint of sexual immorality, or of any kind of impurity, or of greed, because these are improper for God's holy people. Nor should there be obscenity, foolish talk or coarse joking, which are out of place, but rather thanksgiving" (Ephesians 5:3–4).

It is sad that many employ impure, filthy, and crude language in resources designed to help people fight sexual immorality. We cannot attain purity and morality by using language that is impure and immoral. Yes, it is important to speak frankly about sin—to "be real" about the sins we commit and the temptations we face. However, it is possible to be frank without being filthy. With this in mind, I want to promise you I will use no language that is vulgar, crude, impure, or otherwise filthy in this book. As a father of three

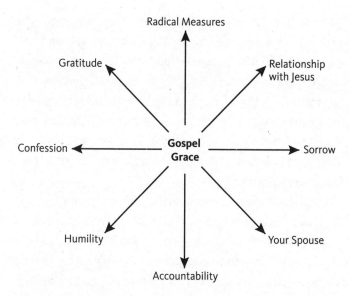

young children, I want to write a book that, should they ever need to read it, would not embarrass me and would not tempt them to impurity. I hope you will have similar confidence in reading this book and in commending it to others.

This book begins with the foundation of grace. Every chapter after the first one explains another essential step in being free from pornography. Please don't think the book starts with grace in chapter 1 and then moves on to other things in the subsequent chapters. Grace is the force that motivates and empowers *every* strategy in the book. The diagram above illustrates how every strategy is founded and dependent on grace.

Every strategy you employ in your fight for purity must be grounded in the grace of God in Christ if it is to lead to lasting freedom. In this vein, I have a recommendation about how to read this book.

Chapter 1 deals with the foundation of the gospel, because no strategy to combat sin can bring profound and lasting change if it is disconnected from the power of Jesus. Strategies are important, but they must flow from the gospel. If you are trying to help a person who is struggling with pornography, it will be wise to read this book all the way through before helping that person. Doing so will give you a sense that practical strategies must flow out of principled commitment to the gospel.

If you are personally struggling with pornography, it is fine to read this book from beginning to end. It may be a good idea, however, to begin with chapter 4's teaching about radical measures before returning to the beginning to read from there. Some of you will be so submerged in a pornographic lifestyle that the gospel teaching at the beginning will best take root *after* you have taken some steps to remove porn from your life. Taking steps like the ones suggested in chapter 4 will never be the long-term fix for your struggle, but doing so can create some space for you to be able to consider the gospel.

This book is for everyone who needs help in the struggle against pornography. Even though I have never met most of you, I know you. I have sat with you in your living room, warned you of the dangers of the sin you are committing, cried with you in your brokenness over that sin, and walked with you in your journey toward change. I know you desire to be finally free from the bondage of pornography. My prayer is that this book will help you fight for purity with the power of grace.

# CHAPTER 1

# Grace as the Foundation in the Fight against Pornography

Matt is a nineteen-year-old college student who discovered pornography at the age of eight when his uncle showed him a video and told him not to tell anybody. Taylor is thirty and never even thought about pornography until succumbing to the temptation of an advertisement in a hotel room on a trip out of town. Ethan has been married for ten years and saw a report on the news about the pornography industry one evening. His curiosity was piqued, and he searched the Internet "just to see what all the fuss was about." Sarah is a single thirty-five-year-old who began looking at pornography as a way to fantasize and get her mind off her loneliness.

I know dozens of people (men and women) who struggle with pornography. Each was introduced to pornography in a different way. Some people sought it out, while others were introduced to it by sinful people. Regardless, pornography has now chewed them up and spit them out. At the beginning of the journey, watching people commit acts of sexual immorality seemed fun, intriguing, comforting, and exhilarating. Now, the sin has bitten back hard. Their hearts are weighed down with guilt, their relationships are strained, their view of sex is corrupted, and their Christian witness is marred.

I know these people. They are my brothers and sisters in Christ. I have sat with them, cried with them, and talked with them for hours. I have seen firsthand the carnage that pornography has inflicted on their lives. Perhaps you or someone God has given to you to help can identify with their stories.

Perhaps you, like them, began to look at pornography with rationalizations that made a certain amount of twisted sense at the time. *How bad can it be? It's just this once, then never again. My spouse doesn't seem that interested in me. It might actually help our marriage for me to have another sexual outlet. I'm sick of feeling lonely. I deserve this.* Now, the sandy foundation holding up those lies has eroded, and you are in turmoil. You desperately want help to get out of the mess, but you don't know how—or even where to begin. In fact, you are deeply afraid you're so trapped that there may be no means of escape.

If this describes you, then I have breathtakingly good news to offer: Jesus Christ died to set you free from every sin that can be committed. That includes pornography.

> But now apart from the law the righteousness of God has been made known, to which the Law and the Prophets testify. This righteousness is given through faith in Jesus Christ to all who believe. There is no difference between Jew and Gentile, for all have sinned

and fall short of the glory of God, and all are justified freely by his grace through the redemption that came by Christ Jesus. God presented Christ as a sacrifice of atonement, through the shedding of his blood—to be received by faith. He did this to demonstrate his righteousness, because in his forbearance he had left the sins committed beforehand unpunished.

*Romans 3:21–25*

It is possible to be free from pornography. Because of his grace, God sent his Son to pay the just penalty for the sins we all commit. When you believe in God's grace toward you, you get God's righteousness. You can be forgiven and free when you trust in Christ and what he has done for you, no matter how many times you have looked at pornography and how hopeless the struggle can feel. When this seems like it isn't true, it's because you are thinking more about yourself and your porn than you are about Jesus and his grace. You can be free, but freedom requires grace.

It is a wonderful blessing to live in a time and place in which large numbers of Christian leaders and laypeople are focusing on the gospel of Jesus in new, fresh, and powerful ways. Multiple books, sermons, and blogs describe the rich resources of grace that overflow from the good news about Jesus. While this current emphasis is admirable, there is a danger that grace can become a topic we discuss rather than a power we experience. We can never be saturated with too much grace. The danger in our day is taking grace for granted and not considering how to make it practical.

I want to heed my own warning. I don't want to just talk about grace in this book; I want to show you how you can make use of the grace of Jesus in your fight against pornography. In Romans 1:5, Paul writes, "Through [Jesus Christ] we received grace and apostleship to call all the Gentiles to the obedience that comes from faith for his name's sake." Here Paul is teaching that God has given his people grace so that they are able to obey and bring honor to the name of Christ among the nations. Grace is not merely "unmerited favor"—that God has a pleasing disposition toward us; grace is also *power*. Grace is divine strength given to us so we can live in ways that please God. God is calling Christians to obedience in Romans 1:5. He is also promising that we will have the power to accomplish this obedience. God's gift of grace is the power to obey.

I want to show you how to seize two important aspects of God's grace in your struggle against pornography.

## Forgiving Grace

The first thing you absolutely must know about God's powerful grace is that through grace God *forgives our sins*. Listen to what the Bible says about this forgiving grace in Colossians 2:13–14: "When you were dead in your sins and in the uncircumcision of your flesh, God made you alive with Christ. He forgave us all our sins, having canceled the charge of our legal indebtedness, which stood against us and condemned us; he has taken it away, nailing it to the cross."

God describes in shocking terms how we can have these amazing blessings. We have life and forgiveness—but these things do not come cheaply.

Paul gives a sobering illustration of this when he compares the sins we have committed to a credit card bill—a "charge of our legal indebtedness." The sins we commit do not vanish into the air, but are documented and preserved. Just like we must pay our credit card bills to avoid legal penalties, so the record of our sin debt makes demands on us that are legally binding. The legal demand of our sin debt is divine punishment. Sin must be paid for. But here we discover a glorious truth: even though you and I are entirely and solely responsible for our sin debt, God makes provision for the debt himself by nailing that debt to the cross of Christ and satisfying its demands. When Jesus was crucified on the cross, he paid for all of our sin. Every instance of treasuring images of sexual immorality in our hearts, every eager glance at pornography, all of our lustful gawking—everything—is paid for by Jesus in his death for sinners.

## Transforming Grace

The news gets even better. Forgiving grace is only one part of the power Jesus gives. God's powerful grace also gives us *strength to live in new ways*. Forgiving grace is wonderful and essential, but sinners need more than forgiveness. It's not enough that our record of debt is paid; we also need grace to live like Jesus; we need grace that changes us so we can be like him in his holiness and love. In Romans 6:4, Paul declares, "We were therefore buried with [Christ] through baptism into death in order that, just as Christ was raised from the dead through the glory of the Father, we too may live a new life."

Paul is talking about the death and resurrection of Jesus. For all who trust in Jesus, his death and resurrection is also *our* death and resurrection. Jesus' death and resurrection not only pays off our record of debt and gives us forgiving grace; Jesus' death and resurrection leads to our transformation.

Through God's transforming grace we can live a new life because of what Jesus has done for us.

Many people spend a lot of time pursuing forgiveness. They beg and plead for forgiveness after indulging in pornography, but they don't know what to do next. The Bible teaches that in addition to confessing sin and seeking God's forgiveness, you need to pursue God's powerful transforming grace by believing the good news and walking in faith and obedience to the gospel. God's grace pardons you and forgives your sin, and God's grace empowers you to live differently and be obedient to him.

Oh, how you must treasure the sweetness of this grace! You need to ask for forgiving grace after you look at pornography, but don't stop there! Ask for God's transforming grace, his power to change you from the inside out. Because God is faithful to his Word and his promises, over time you will receive God's power to never look at pornography again. God's powerful transforming grace *can* give you a pure heart, and you *can* subdue your desires for pornography. You *can* honor your brothers and sisters in Christ when you look at them instead of dishonoring them. You can have all of this, and more. You just can't get it in your own strength and effort. You need the powerful transforming grace of Jesus.

God's powerful transforming grace is available to you, but many people don't know how to make use of it. Having the power of Jesus to change without knowing how to use that power is almost like not having the power at all. It's like being stranded on an island with a fueled-up airplane you don't know how to fly. It is crucial to discover how to grasp God's grace if you are going to benefit from it. If you want to use Jesus' transforming grace, you have to do something so easy that many people find it impossible.

You have to *believe* it.

Transforming grace works when you believe that Jesus gives it to you. The moment you believe in Jesus' grace to change you, you *are* changing. The more you continue to believe it, the more you will continue to change.

Paul writes, "In the same way, count yourselves dead to sin but alive to God in Christ Jesus" (Romans 6:11). Paul is saying that you are dead to sin and alive to God in Christ when you *count* it to be true; that is, when you believe it. If you want to change and be like Christ—whether in the area of pornography or anything else—you must believe that in Jesus you have the power to change. When you believe the power is yours, it is yours.

## Repentance and Grace

Forgiving grace and transforming grace are crucial for Christians to embrace. Repentance is the way we grasp and unite these two essential aspects of God's grace. In the aftermath of sin, we must learn to interact with God through repentance. In the Bible, repentance describes the process of moving from sinful living to obedient living. When we repent, we must always take at least three clear steps. You can remember these three essential steps by using the acronym CAR.

The first step in the process of repentance is to *confess* your sin. The apostle John writes, "If we claim to be without sin, we deceive ourselves and the truth is not in us. If we confess our sins, he is faithful and just and will forgive us our sins and purify us from all unrighteousness" (1 John 1:8–9). Sinners need grace more than anything else, including the grace to recognize and admit our sin. We reject grace when we deny our sin, according to John. When you deny your sin, you deny yourself access to God's grace. When you admit your sin to God, you access his grace. The first step in repentance is to talk to God and tell him about your sin. He already knows this, of course, but we still need to tell God about the sin we are aware of in our life. In a marriage, when a husband has an angry outburst and speaks harshly to his wife, he must still admit his wrong and seek forgiveness— even though she experienced it and knows it happened. In the same way, every Christian who struggles with sexual immorality needs to humble himself or herself before God, telling God what he already knows.

The second step in the process of repentance is to *affirm* God's forgiveness of your sin. John provides two directions to follow (see 1 John 1:8–9). First, he gives a command to obey: you must confess your sins. Second, he gives a message to believe: when you confess your sin, God is faithful to forgive and cleanse you. It is easier to talk to God about your sin than it is to believe you are forgiven. Perhaps this is your struggle.

You may find yourself thinking about all the pornographic images you've seen, the lustful heart you've nurtured, or the number of people broken by your immorality. These sorrows are part of the consequence of sin. When you dwell disproportionately on your sin and its consequences, however, you are neglecting God's grace. There is a time and a place to be broken over your sin and to soberly consider its consequences (the next chapter is devoted to this topic). After you have confessed your sin, however, you must fight to affirm what God says about you. For all who confess their sin, God pronounces the verdict "forgiven" and "clean." If God pronounces you forgiven and clean, you *are* forgiven and clean. While it may seem humble and modest to question God's forgiveness, it is actually prideful and arrogant to refuse to believe what God declares to be true about you. Repentance means affirming what God says about you.

The third step in the process of repentance is to *request* Jesus' grace to change. We have already seen the amazing power available to Christians in the work of Jesus. We must also recognize the biblical warning that is too often true of us as prayerless followers of Jesus: "You do not have because you do not ask God" (James 4:2). Having confessed your sin and trusted in God's forgiveness, you now need to ask God for the specific grace to be different.

It is important to talk about repentance because repentance is the means by which you lay hold of Jesus' forgiving and transforming grace. It is possible to talk about how grace forgives and transforms us but never actually experience those graces. God does not just want us to know about these graces; he wants us to live them out. The way we practically live, experience, and are transformed by the grace of Jesus is to talk to God about it. Asking for and believing in God's forgiveness of our sin and his power to change us is essential to experiencing it.

Knowing this changes the way we will respond to failure in the battle against pornography. We typically respond to moral failures with mental punishments. You've probably experienced this. You sin and look at pornography. Then you start thinking, *I'm terrible. I'm awful. What was I thinking? If my friends knew what I was doing, they would never talk to me again. I can never be in ministry if I don't quit doing this. What if my spouse finds out? What if my girlfriend finds out? What if my parents find out? What if my pastor finds out? What if people at church find out? I don't deserve to be a Christian. Maybe I'm not a Christian.* On and on and on it goes. You cycle through these mental punishments that grow out of guilt and fuel even more guilt.

None of this is helpful, but it's what most people do in their struggle with pornography and lust. Mental punishments are not helpful because they deal with sin in a self-centered way instead of a Christ-centered way. Meditating on how miserable and pathetic you are only perpetuates the sinful self-centeredness that led you to look at pornography in the first place. Condemning self-talk still has you standing center stage as you reflect on what you think about what you have done, and as you describe what you think you deserve because of what you did. It's all about you. The problem is there is too much you in all this. You need Christ. And the only way to break the vicious cycle is to get outside of yourself to Jesus. You need to stop talking to yourself in categories of condemnation and begin talking to God in categories of confession.

What I just shared with you is a big deal. You should pay attention to it and reread it if you didn't catch it. As the Lord sets you free from the sin of pornography, this will be one of the biggest changes he will make in your life. You will learn to stop responding to pornography by talking to yourself with condemning words and thoughts and start responding to your sin by talking to God with prayers of confession. Self-talk and self-condemnation do nothing to lay hold of God's forgiving and transforming grace. Repentance does.

The tide will begin to turn in your struggle against pornography when you begin to grasp forgiving grace *and* transforming grace, as you learn to repent. To experience freedom, you must repent. You will need to come to Christ in your brokenness, frustration, disgust, and shame. You must talk to him about it. Tell him what you did. Tell him what you were thinking and wanting. Be honest. Cry and ask him to forgive you. Ask him for grace to be different. As you do this, you are moving away from trusting in yourself as the solution to your sin and approaching the throne of grace where Jesus is ready to respond with mercy to help you in your time of need (Hebrews 4:16).

## Hope and Grace

God's grace gives birth to hope. There is a good chance you've picked up this book in despair. Perhaps you recently indulged in pornography for the zillionth time and have finally had enough. Perhaps a spouse, parent, coworker, or law enforcement authority discovered your secret indulgence and now you're in trouble at home, church, or work, or with the law. Regardless of your exact circumstances, you're despairing that change can ever be possible.

It's not as though despair is unreasonable. It makes sense to despair as you look at a devastating problem that has hooked millions of people before you and will trap millions more after you. It makes sense to despair as you look at life-altering consequences—a broken relationship with the Lord, a damaged relationship with your spouse, suspicions from your children, parents, or friends, and a lost job or ministry position. It makes sense to despair as you look within and see a total inability to change by means of your own resources. There are many legitimate reasons to despair when you consider these bleak realities.

The logic of despair is broken by the miracle of grace. The power of God melts despair when you grasp his forgiving and transforming grace through repentance. Pornography is a plague that has destroyed countless lives and can also destroy yours. The sobering truth is that you do not have the resources to change within yourself.

"*But where sin increased, grace increased all the more*" (Romans 5:20).

No matter how terrible pornography is, no matter how much trouble you are in, no matter how flimsy and weak your resources are, you are never in a pit so deep that the grace of Jesus cannot lift you out. The great danger in your struggle is that you will devote all of your energy to thinking true and awful things about pornography and spend no time dwelling on the true and wonderful things about Jesus.

There is no porn user so enslaved that Jesus cannot set him or her free. There is no struggle for purity so intense that Jesus' grace cannot win the battle. There is no consequence so steep that Jesus' power cannot carry you through. Jesus' grace to change you is stronger than pornography's power to destroy you. Jesus' grace is stronger than your own desires to watch sex. While there is no hope for you in looking at pornography, there is all the hope in the universe when you look to God and his grace.

Hope for lasting transformation begins when you cry out to God in repentance and plead with him for his forgiving and transforming grace. When you ask for these things in faith, *he will never deny them to you.* This prayer is the very first step you must take as you turn away from pornography. God's grace is available to you right now. Do not turn the page until you sense that you have encountered God's grace in repentance. When you are ready to turn the page, I will begin to unfold eight practical elements of God's transforming grace that he delights to grant to his loved ones who ask.

# Fighting for Purity with the Power of Grace

1. Pray to God right now and confess your sin of looking at pornography. Seek God's forgiving grace from this sin.

2. As you pray, ask God for his powerful transforming grace to bring change to your life.

3. Don't stop praying until you truly believe that these graces are yours in Christ.

# CHAPTER 2

# Using Sorrow to Fight Pornography

Ryan sat in my office sobbing. Not crying, but sobbing. His hands were busy wiping oceans of tears from his face as he wailed confessions of sin and regret. His wife sat beside him with a face so hard it looked like it was chiseled in granite. Ryan and Lisa had been married for fifteen years and had three kids. They were meeting with me because their decade and a half of marriage was filled with Ryan's love for pornography. After years of repeated discoveries, Lisa's initial discouragement had spiraled into despair, and now her despair had twisted into disdain. Lisa was finished—she wanted to take the kids and get far away from Ryan. Ryan's moaning and pleading for her to remain with him were so desperate and loud that it attracted the attention of people down the hall.

Dave had a similar story. He had been married to Marie for twenty years. He had periodically dabbled in pornography, buying a magazine every now and then. In the last year, though, he had discovered pornography on the Internet. When introduced to the ease and anonymity of viewing pornography on the web, Dave became totally enslaved. He spent hours looking at it and eventually became disinterested in his wife. Marie knew something was different but was not prepared when she discovered her husband was hooked on porn. Horrified, she left their house to stay with a friend. Like Ryan, Dave pleaded with loud tears for Marie to forgive him. He begged for forgiveness. He swore he would change. He vowed never to look at pornography again. He wept on his knees, crying at Marie's feet in total brokenness.

Dave and Ryan do not know each other, but they have a lot in common. Both have serious problems with pornography and have had for some time. Both are "family men" with a wife and children. Both stand to lose their family because of their sin. Both are in desperate situations as they cry and plead for reconciliation.

I know Dave and Ryan, and I know how their stories play out. I can tell you that only one of them really changed. Only one of these men is reconciled to his wife and restored to a happy, porn-free life with his family. The other is now divorced from his wife and totally separated from his kids. One of them is restored and living a happy life with his family and is not looking at pornography. One of them was interested in real change on that day; the other was not. Which one do you think changed?

It's hard to tell, isn't it? Both men were heartbroken. Both were sincere. Both displayed an apparent commitment to their family. Both appeared willing to do whatever it took to change their sinful lifestyle. In spite of their outward similarities, these two men are as different as cats and dogs. Though they both displayed sorrow, their tears were drawn from two totally different wells.

## Two Kinds of Sorrow

In a letter the apostle Paul wrote to Christians in the city of Corinth, he helps us understand the difference between the two men. Paul had a complicated relationship with the Corinthians. They were sinning in numerous ways and being led astray by false teachers, and it was Paul's job to rebuke them and call them to faithfulness. These corrective measures produced some firm statements from Paul and led to a sorrowful response from the Corinthians. After the Corinthians began to be restored to Christ, Paul wrote these words to them about the sadness they experienced along the way.

> Even if I caused you sorrow by my letter, I do not regret it. Though I did regret it—I see that my letter hurt you, but only for a little while—yet now I am happy, not because you were made sorry, but because your sorrow led you to repentance. For you became sorrowful as God intended and so were not harmed in any way by us. Godly sorrow brings repentance that leads to salvation and leaves no regret, but worldly sorrow brings death. See what this godly sorrow has produced in you: what earnestness, what eagerness to clear yourselves, what indignation, what alarm, what longing, what concern, what readiness to see justice done. At every point you have proved yourselves to be innocent in this matter.
>
> *2 Corinthians 7:8–11*

Paul makes a distinction between two kinds of sorrow in this passage. These two sorrows possess different traits and produce opposite results, but we easily confuse them because they share the most obvious element—the sorrow itself. We rarely question deep remorse, stinging regret, or impassioned pleas for forgiveness. Paul knows better than this. By using a comparison, he shows the Corinthians that all sorrow is not created equal.

One kind of sorrow Paul talks about is worldly sorrow. Worldly sorrow is legitimate sorrow. There is actual sadness, brokenness, and tears when a person experiences this kind of sorrow. The issue is not whether a person is sad; instead, it is what they are sad *about*. The focus of worldly sorrow is the world. People experiencing worldly sorrow are distressed because they are losing (or fear losing) things the world has to offer. The loss could be a reputation, job, money, family, sexual fulfillment, or even access to pornography—anything that brings security, comfort, or pleasure. Some of these things are good, and some of these things are sinful, but they are all *things*. A sad person consumed with worldly sorrow is concerned about losing stuff—no matter how honorable or dishonorable that stuff is.

This kind of worldly sorrow leads to death. It is lethal because it flows from the same kind of heart that wanted to look at pornography in the first place. This connection is critical for you to understand. A sinful heart that desires to look at pornography says, *I will have whatever I want whenever I want it. I don't care if it's harmful, if it hurts God or those I love. I will have whatever I want.* This kind of heart sins in pursuit of its own pleasures. Worldly sorrow is obsessed with keeping these objects of selfish desire. All the tears and all the pain are actually about the loss of your stuff. You're crying about the things you're about to lose and would like to keep. You looked at pornography because you were living life for yourself. Now you're sad because you're about to lose stuff that you would like to keep. The self-centered orientation of your heart is the same, whether you're lustfully viewing pornography or tearfully expressing worldly sorrow. It is terrifying to think that even our sorrow over sin can be selfish and sinful.

There is another kind of sorrow. Paul calls it godly sorrow. It may look just as sad as the worldly variety, but something very different is happening in the heart. Worldly sorrow is sad over losing the things of the world, while the focus of godly sorrow is God himself. Godly sorrow is pained over the break in relationship with God. It is heartbroken that God has been grieved and offended. The tears of godly sorrow flow from the sadness that God's loving and holy law has been broken. Of course, there is room in godly sorrow for the loss of family, hurt relationships, or other consequences. You do not have to love the practical consequences of sin. Yet, the pain of these penalties is not what produces godly sorrow; godly sorrow is motivated by and oriented toward God.

Godly sorrow produces repentance leading to salvation without regret. Godly sorrow produces life. It marks a change from the sinful self-centeredness of viewing porn and the equal self-centeredness of worldly sorrow to a pure concern for God and living for his glory. The person full of godly sorrow has a heart that wants to please God rather than self. Godly sorrow motivates real and lasting change.

Though Ryan and Dave both look sorrowful on the outside, very different things are happening on the inside, in their hearts. It is a distinction that has everything to do with you and your own struggle to be free from the grip of pornography. By the time you're reading a book like this, there is a very good chance you have produced tears by the quart in your struggle. The pressing question for you is not whether Ryan and Dave have worldly or godly sorrow. The most important question is, which sorrow do you have? How can you know if your tears stem from concern over the world or concern over God?

## The Marks of Godly Sorrow

This is where 2 Corinthians 7:8–11 becomes even more practical. Paul not only highlights a difference between lifeless sorrow and life-giving sorrow but also describes in detail how you can tell the difference. He mentions six different markers for godly sorrow.

### 1. Godly Sorrow Is Earnest.

Worldly sorrow experiences sin, winces at the pain, and feels conviction—for a while. Worldly sorrow responds to that conviction by praying—for a while. Worldly sorrow is really determined to fight against sin—for a while. The problem is that this newfound conviction, this rededication to prayer, and this emotional determination are all short-lived. The pain of what you have lost (or the fear of what you might lose) fades away. You figure out that you can live without what you lost or else replace it with something else. Once this realization hits, your sorrow disappears like breath on a cold winter morning.

Godly sorrow is not short-lived. Instead, it is earnest. Godly sorrow gets busy and fervently seeks to fight against sin in a battle that lasts and lasts. Biblical remorse over sin extends far beyond a momentary wince of pain and a fleeting twinge of conviction. Godly sorrow is busy battling pornography weeks, months, and years after worldly sorrow has given up the struggle. If the sorrow you experience after your struggle with pornography does not lead to real and lasting transformation, then you've experienced worldly sorrow and you stand in desperate need of change.

## 2. Godly Sorrow Leads to an Eagerness to Clear Yourself.

When your sorrow flows from a heart oriented toward God rather than yourself, you will be eager to clear yourself from the sin of pornography. Worldly sorrow leaves and is quickly replaced by a renewed interest in porn. You find yourself on the pathway to indulgence again. Godly sorrow longs to be clear of pornography and eagerly pursues ways to eradicate it.

Eagerness to be clear of pornography expresses itself in two practical ways. First, you pursue accountability. You need help in a struggle that is impossible to fight alone. Accountability entails enlisting other Christians who can help you think about strategies you have not considered, who can actively check up on you, and who will diligently pray for you. Second, eagerly seeking to clear yourself means you pursue radical measures to ensure you have no access to pornography. This enslaving sin is only defeated by drastic measures to cut it off from all angles.

Accountability and drastic measures will be discussed in greater detail in later chapters. For now, know that if your sorrow does not lead to opening yourself up to others and sealing off your access to pornography, then your sorrow is the kind of worldly sorrow that leads to death.

### 3. Godly Sorrow Leads to Indignation.

Godly sorrow produces indignation. It produces hatred. Worldly sorrow produces hatred, but it is directed at other things. Worldly sorrow hates the consequences of sin. The tears of worldly sorrow spring from shame over a lost job or ministry, disgust over a spouse who thinks you're creepy, embarrassment over being disciplined by your school or parents, or some other painful result of sin. The hatred of worldly sorrow is the hatred of being caught.

Godly sorrow hates the sin itself. Godly sorrow feels the horror of disobedience and weeps over the reality of a heart that chose transgression over faithfulness. The painful grief of life-giving sorrow is produced by the stinging awareness that all sin breaks God's heart, even if no one else ever discovers it. Worldly sorrow is sad because people know about your sin. Godly sorrow is sad because God knows about your sin. Worldly sorrow is sad because of a disrupted relationship with a spouse, kids, or others. Godly sorrow is sad because of a disrupted relationship with God. Sorrow is lethal when self-focused. We must repent and say with David, "Against you, you only, have I sinned" (Psalm 51:4).

### 4. Godly Sorrow Leads to Alarm.

Godly sorrow produces alarm, a healthy form of fear. Worldly sorrow also produces alarm, but it is misdirected. The fear of worldly sorrow is the fear that people will find out. In worldly sorrow you didn't get earnest and you haven't been eager to clear yourself from the sin. You may have made a show of change, but the substance never came. It didn't take too long for you to go right back to looking at all the same stuff you looked at before. Now you're living in fear that people will find out—or find out again—that you aren't for real. All your effort is spent on not being caught. You're trying to hide in the dark instead of exposing the darkness to light. This will never lead to lasting change.

Godly sorrow doesn't fear that people will find out about your sin. Rather, you fear that God—the only person who ultimately matters—always knew. I am a very sinful man in great need of the blood of Jesus to forgive me for all the ways I have failed God. When I consider the ways I have continued to sin as a Christian, I see the arrogance in my heart and am aware of the damage I do to myself in that sin. I feel the pain I bring to others because of my sin, and my heart breaks over the disappointment my sin brings to God. Though I am sinful, God is full of perfection and purity. He can't stand to look on the selfishness and impurity of sin. I'm astounded that God lets me live during those seasons of sinfulness. Though I defy him, he gives me breath, food, shelter, and countless other gifts. Godly sorrow recognizes this holy intolerance of sin. It is fear mingled with an awareness of mercy—that God didn't give us the just punishment we deserved.

## 5. Godly Sorrow Leads to Longing and Concern for Restoration.

Godly sorrow is full of longing and concern for restored relationships. Paul praises the Corinthians for their concern to be restored to him after sin had distanced them from each other (2 Corinthians 7:7). Sin separates us from others, bringing division into relationships, creating distance instead of intimacy.

Godly sorrow demonstrates itself by a deep concern to restore the relationships that were broken. Godly sorrow is pained by the wedge of separation that pornography brings between you and God. It longs for restoration. Godly sorrow is broken over the distance your sin has created in relationships with others and longs to close the gap.

Worldly sorrow wants to let bygones be bygones. It preaches about leaving the past in the past and letting sleeping dogs lie. When your tears result in your running away from people instead of toward them, your tears are worldly tears. Worldly grief ignores God instead of leaning more fully on his forgiveness and grows comfortable with broken relationships. Life-giving sorrow infuses you with zeal to restore every single relationship that has been broken. Your sorrow leads you either deeper inside yourself or toward God and others.

## 6. Godly Sorrow Leads to a Desire for Justice.

I once counseled a man named Tyler who began looking at pornography with a mistaken belief that he was in control. He learned the hard way that sin never lets you have control. Sin is a harsh master, not a submissive servant. Over the years, Tyler spent more time looking at more perverse forms of pornography than he ever thought possible. A few weeks before our first meeting, he was arrested for being in possession of child pornography. Tyler needed help changing, but there was a pressing legal question to address.

The arresting officers had made mistakes during the arrest and established a very weak case. Tyler's attorney assured him that if he would go to trial and plead not guilty, he could be easily exonerated. Tyler wondered aloud what I thought he should do. My only question for him was whether or not he was actually in possession of the pornography. He admitted his guilt to me. I told him he could plead not guilty if he wanted to die, but that if he wanted to live, he should plead guilty and accept the consequences. He seemed shocked, until I read him 2 Corinthians 7:8–11. Tyler understood my point and pleaded guilty to his crime.

Doing what is right and just doesn't always make life more comfortable for you. An immediate and critical test for whether your sorrow is godly or worldly is whether you're willing to accept the consequences of your sin. If so, there is a very good chance that your sorrow is the godly kind that saves. If you're trying to wriggle out of consequences, there is a high probability that your sorrow is the worldly kind that is all about you.

*∗ ∗ ∗*

Finally, Paul writes, "At every point you have proved yourselves to be innocent in this matter." This statement could sound like Paul is saying that the Corinthians have proven themselves innocent of sin. Innocence cannot be his focus, however, because Paul is describing their repentance from sin. In showing these marks of godly sorrow, the Corinthians demonstrated themselves to be innocent not of sin but of worldly sorrow. The Corinthians' earnestness, eagerness, indignation, alarm, longing, concern, and desire for justice showed they were not guilty of the kind of sorrow that leads to death. Instead they proved their sorrow had led to repentance and life.

## The Difference between Dave and Ryan

Two men were enslaved to pornography. Each wept over his sin, begged his wife for another chance, pleaded for forgiveness, and vowed to change. But today only one is walking with Christ, devoted to his wife and children, and truly transformed.

Dave was the man who truly changed after the initial meeting in my office and is now fully restored to his family. I'm sorry to say that Ryan ultimately returned to his pornography, eventually began meeting women online, and became a danger to his family. He is now divorced from his wife and not allowed near his children, and he has even spent time in jail because his habit has descended into illegal activity. Dave's tears led to earnestness because they were godly tears. Ryan's tears couldn't sustain real change because he never moved from desiring the things of the world to desiring the things of God.

The big difference between Ryan and Dave—and between worldly and godly sorrow—is God. Worldly sorrow happens when you feel the sting of sin but still cherish a selfish love of sin in your heart. Godly sorrow happens when you are gripped by your sinful separation from God and desire to be restored to him at any cost.

As you fight for purity with the power of grace, you must labor to imitate Dave's godly sorrow. A person full of godly sorrow is a person oriented toward God and has a heart and emotions that are inclined toward him. Worldly sorrow is oriented toward yourself and your love for the securities, comforts, and pleasures of the world.

If you recognize that you have only worldly sorrow, you need radical change. Your heart and your emotions must be oriented away from yourself and toward God and his kingdom. You will never be free from pornography if all your efforts to stop are recycled expressions of your own selfishness. As long as your sorrow is like your sin and focused on the things you want, you will return to porn again and again. Until God is your chief concern—until sinning against him is what makes your heart break—you will never turn the corner.

Whether you are plagued with an absence of sorrow or the presence of worldly sorrow, the solution is the same. You need God's forgiving and transforming grace. You need forgiving grace for having the wrong kind of response to your sin and you need transforming grace to have the kind of broken heart that honors God. Those graces can be yours now, just for the asking. Before you proceed further in reading this book, let me encourage you to seek Christ and ask for his grace to forgive and change you as you fight for godly sorrow.

# Fighting for Purity with the Power of Grace

1. Spend some time in honest reflection, asking whether you have been sorrowful in your struggle with pornography. If so, what have you been sorrowful over? Is your sadness over the consequences of being caught or over the break in your relationship with God? Ask God to help you be honest in your answer. Be aware that if you've had an ongoing struggle with pornography, your sorrow is likely worldly. Write down the real reasons for your sadness.

2. Spend time in prayer asking for Christ's forgiving grace for your worldly sorrow or for the absence of sorrow. Ask for Christ's transforming grace to fill your heart with godly sorrow over your sin of looking at pornography. Believe that as you trust in Christ, he will give you what you ask for.

3. To fuel your godly sorrow, meditate on passages of Scripture such as Psalm 25; Psalm 32; and Titus 2:11–15. Consider what these passages teach about the goodness of God and the horror of sin. Ask God to help you feel the weight of the damage your sin does to your relationship with God.

# CHAPTER 3

# Using Accountability to Fight Pornography

It was one of those beautiful afternoons in early fall when a crisp breeze in the air and a cup of hot coffee in your hand make it just comfortable enough to sit outside. I was waiting on the patio of a local coffee shop for a church member who had asked to speak with me. I didn't know what was on his mind, but as I waited I prayed that I could serve him in some way. Ben arrived, and after some small talk, he got straight to the point. He was in a losing battle with pornography.

Ben was trying really hard to defeat his sin, but sincere effort had combined with sparse victory to produce serious discouragement. His former college pastor had insisted he find a group of guys to hold him accountable. Ben followed this good advice and had been faithfully meeting with two guys every week since. Every guy in the group sensed that their efforts in the battle against porn had stalled, with no real victory. My friend fought off tears, looking for an explanation for his frequent failure. Why was change eluding him when he was doing exactly what his pastor had told him to do?

## The Importance of Accountability

The Bible is clear that believers need accountability. Listen to the words of Paul in Galatians: "Brothers and sisters, if someone is caught in a sin, you who live by the Spirit should restore that person gently. But watch yourselves, or you also may be tempted. Carry each other's burdens, and in this way you will fulfill the law of Christ (Galatians 6:1–2).

The word *accountability* is not found in this passage, but the text teaches two crucial lessons about our need for others in the fight against sin. First, if you are caught in a sin, you need to be restored by someone who lives by the Spirit. We are not designed to pull our way out of our spiritual ruts in our own strength. We need the help of other Christians. You will never be free from pornography until you acknowledge that in order to change you need the help of God through brothers and sisters in Christ.

Second, this passage speaks to you if you are in the position of providing accountability for someone else. Paul instructs spiritual mentors to restore struggling persons in a spirit of gentleness and love. When we think of accountability, we often think of someone foolish and weak who is in need of someone wise and strong. However, Paul also teaches that people who are spiritually mature need the struggling persons they are helping. Jesus commands spiritual mentors to carry each other's burdens and thus fulfill the law of Christ. Wise mentors need struggling persons in order to obey that command.

You may be reading this book, not as someone who struggles with pornography, but as one called to help a friend or loved one who faces this challenge. You need to guard your heart carefully against the feelings of frustration and annoyance that can occur when you are helping someone whose struggle is different from your own. The Word of God tells us that we should help to carry the burdens of those who are weaker and struggling in the battles against sin. Never forget that everyone—even if they are not struggling with this particular sin—will need help at some point. It may not be long before you need the kind of help from others that they are asking from you. Be gracious and understanding as you deal with your struggling brother or sister.

Accountability is an essential element in the fight for purity and freedom from pornography. The Bible is clear that we need each other, whether we are the one who is caught in a transgression or the person restoring one who is. Sinners and those helping to carry their burdens need each other as they grow to be more like Christ. As Ben and I talked on that cool day, we discovered a number of problems in Ben's battle against pornography. The problem was *not* his understanding of his need for accountability. Ben simply needed to understand how to use accountability more effectively than he had been. I believe there are seven principles that can help strengthen the common weakness we find in most accountability relationships, enabling them to work the way God intended them to work.

## 1. Effective Accountability Doesn't Rely Exclusively on Accountability.

Ben's meeting with this group of guys was the *only* thing he was doing to fight against porn. As important as that is, it's not enough. In other chapters, you will learn about other strategies that are needed to win the battle. Too often, people who struggle with pornography use accountability as the only weapon in their arsenal against porn. While it is an important weapon, accountability is only one weapon among many. No matter how frequent the meetings, how open the confession, or how encouraging the group, Ben needed to broaden his approach in order to kill his sin and counter his temptation on each and every front. Limiting your weapons unnecessarily limits victory. This book points to numerous other resources Christ has given you.

## 2. Effective Accountability Is Involved Early Rather Than Late.

Perhaps your accountability meetings are similar to how Ben described his. After the group opens with prayer, Ben goes first. Everyone asks Ben how he did during the past week. He winces. "Well, guys, I didn't do so well. The fact is, I looked at pornography twice this week." Everyone expresses their sorrow and promises to pray.

Steve is up next. Anticipating the question, he confesses apologetically, "I'm like Ben this week. I feel terrible, but I actually looked at pornography four times this week." Again, there's expression of regret all around. Everyone feels badly for Steve and tells him so. They promise to pray for him, and he believes they really will.

Now it's Nathan's turn. As Steve and Ben wait to hear this third report, Nathan breaks the silence with a nervous chuckle. "Guys I'm no better than you. I had a pretty good week, but last night I gave in and looked at pornography for almost an hour." The other guys can tell Nathan is particularly discouraged and put comforting hands on his shoulders.

They assure him he is not alone in the battle and remind him of the payment Jesus made for his sin. They conclude with prayer, encouraging one another to be strong and agreeing to meet the same time next week.

What is wrong with this meeting? Sadly, this well-intentioned conversation illustrates several defective approaches to accountability. One of those defective approaches is that these guys are only reporting on the sin they have already committed rather than asking for help to battle the temptations that precede sin. In other words, they are waiting until the end of the week to talk about all the pornography they looked at instead of calling out for help during the week—while they are tempted and before they actually sin.

Many accountability groups function as an opportunity for a delayed confession of sin. You must change this pattern if you want to be free from porn. You must begin to reach out to your accountability partners when you are tempted instead of waiting for a meeting to confess your sins after the fact. Here is a crucial truth for you to consider: *You will not experience dramatic change in your struggle as long as you use accountability to describe your sins instead of declaring your need for help in the midst of temptation.* You must ask Jesus for grace and agree with those holding you accountable that you will call for help as soon as you realize you're being tempted. Anyone who waits for the scheduled meeting to report their sins needs encouragement to engage the struggle earlier.

## 3. Effective Accountability Involves Someone with Maturity.

Another defective approach of the meeting Ben described is that, despite their sincere intentions, these young men are all at the same level of maturity and entangled in the same sin. No one in the group has the spiritual stability to counterbalance their communal confusion. None of these guys have the proven wisdom to correct their collective waywardness. No one who has experienced lasting victory is there to guide the group out of long-standing defeat. You must have someone providing leadership in your accountability group who is more advanced in holiness than the others.

We see in Galatians 6:1–2 that those caught in sins are restored by those who live by the Spirit. Living by the Spirit doesn't imply "perfect." No Christian will meet that ultimate standard until they see Jesus face-to-face. This passage does indicate, however, that you need someone more advanced than yourself in the area of your struggle. Seeking accountability from those who are in the same place in their struggle as you are may make you feel comfortable but is unlikely to lead to actual change. You must be accountable to someone who has a track record of victory in sexual purity. This kind of person is best equipped to point you toward freedom in your own life.

## 4. Effective Accountability Involves Someone with Authority.

It is crucial to be accountable to someone with more maturity, but you must go one step further. You must also be accountable to someone with spiritual authority to help you change. If you wonder what I mean, look at Hebrews 13:17: "Have confidence in your leaders and submit to their authority, because they keep watch over you as those who must give an account." God has provided his people with leaders who possess spiritual authority. We are called to follow these spiritual leaders because they are overseeing and protecting our souls. They will answer directly to God for how they fulfill their responsibility.

Such leaders have a number of tools in their accountability toolbox that other mature Christians do not have. One tool is the ability to make appeals based on their objective and God-given spiritual authority. It's more sobering to be called to repentance by a pastor than by a person in your community group. This difference is not related to any distinction in personal worth. Rather, God has given more spiritual authority to spiritual leaders.

Spiritual leaders also possess the ability to lead the entire church to correct members who refuse to repent of persistent sinful patterns. God has instituted a process for calling to repentance Christians who are caught in a pit of sin. First, they are to be confronted by an individual, then by several Christians together, and then by the entire church (Matthew 18:15 – 20). The rebellious church member can repent at any of these three steps. If they refuse, Jesus says they are to be removed from the church. Spiritual leaders are equipped to initiate this formal process in a way that other Christians are not.

Church discipline, as this process is often called, is a kind of accountability all its own. Christians who love Christ and love being associated with his church will be more diligent to fight against pornography rather than face formal correction and discipline by those in their church.

Our weakened Christian culture often views this kind of accountability as unloving or authoritarian. Many groups do this kind of thing, however. Businesses hold their employees accountable to their corporate values and standards of conduct. Honorable sports teams are often known for "policing the locker room." Civic organizations enforce ethical requirements among their membership. If the surrounding culture is willing to impose their rules, how much more should the church and her members be devoted to this when the very Word of God is at stake!

If you have never confessed your sin to one of the spiritual authorities in your church, you are cutting yourself off from a crucial source of spiritual help. You need them if you are as serious as you should be about being set free from the grip of pornography.

## 5. Effective Accountability Should Avoid Explicit Details.

The recommendations in this chapter are meant to improve the effectiveness of accountability relationships, but this particular recommendation does more than improve effectiveness—it actually keeps conversations from becoming a disaster. The unfortunate truth is that when people share their struggles in a graphic way, it can intensify temptations. Sadly, it is possible for an accountability conversation that was intended for good to become something that introduces a struggling sinner to new places and ways to find pornography rather than helping him battle his fleshly desires. Participants in the group can unwisely share explicit details about the kinds of pornography they watch, discuss the characteristics of the actors in the porn they view, or identify where they located their porn. Unnecessary details like these can turn accountability from a helpful context for finding freedom into a harmful place for fueling temptation.

Pay attention to Paul's wisdom when he writes, "Have nothing to do with the fruitless deeds of darkness, but rather expose them. It is shameful even to mention what the disobedient do in secret" (Ephesians 5:11–12). There is a wonderful tension in these verses. On the one hand, Paul encourages you to expose your unfruitful works of darkness, the sexual sins you have committed. On the other hand, he says that it is shameful even to speak of the dark deeds done in secret. In other words, you are to expose the shameful works of darkness but not speak of them. That's quite a tension! How are you to do both?

You will balance these two truths by describing enough of your struggle that those helping you know how to keep you accountable but not giving so much detail that it would fuel further temptation. Your accountability partner needs to know, in broad terms, how you access pornography (for example, they need to know if you seek it out on the Internet or buy it from a store). They need to know approximately how much time you spend viewing pornography, and if you're looking at styles of pornography that are different from what they might expect. For example, you should make it clear if you are watching homosexual pornography, child pornography, or other types that indicate a specific kind of struggle beyond viewing acts of more typical sexual immorality. The wisest approach is to describe particular temptations in general terms. You cross a biblical line when you give detailed descriptions of the scenes you've viewed or explain the specifics of where you located your porn.

## 6. Effective Accountability Places the Responsibility for Confession on the Person with the Problem.

There are all sorts of accountability questions floating around out there that spiritual mentors are supposed to ask those they're seeking to help. They begin with questions like: *Did you look at pornography this week? Did you make any attempt to look at pornography this week?* The questions continue until the final one—the fail-safe question—is asked: *Did you lie to me in any of your answers?* There's nothing inherently wrong with these questions when an accountability relationship is just starting out. It's a bad idea, however, to continue in this way for very long. Accountability oriented around questions and answers can devolve into a cat-and-mouse game in which the struggler provides legally precise answers that are something less than a full and open disclosure of sin. Even when the confession is totally honest, what gets confessed can easily be limited to the question asked.

The responsibility to confess sin and expose the darkness lies with the person who has committed the sin. It's not the job of spiritual mentors to go on a fishing expedition to reel in a confession from those they are trying to help. A person passively waiting to provide answers to specific questions is in a far different place spiritually than a person who is willing to take the initiative to expose their struggles in the pure light of day. In other words, keep the responsibility where it belongs and simply invite the person to share where they have sinned and need help. This will reveal just how much help a person looking at pornography really wants. Accountability leads to freedom much more quickly when conversations grow into times of honest and free confession on the part of the struggler. Spiritual mentors can certainly begin with questions to start the conversation, but they should also keep in mind the goal—full and free confession without the prompting of questions or probing to uncover hidden secrets.

## 7. Effective Accountability Must Actually Hold People Accountable.

One final correction you may need to make in your accountability relationship is finding someone with the desire and the ability actually to hold you accountable. In many groups there is a lot of reporting but no real accountability. Ben, Nathan, and Steve have no way of knowing whether the other guys in their group are telling the truth. It wouldn't be at all surprising, for example, to discover that Steve looked at pornography ten times instead of the four he confessed. We don't have to assume that Steve lied, but guys who look at porn often do. The point is that nobody really knows. If you're going to hold people accountable, you should *actually hold them accountable*. If you want others to hold you accountable, you should seek out people who will really do it. It's a bad idea just to listen to what people say without discernment, evaluation, and—when necessary—verification.

True accountability involves three elements. First, you need to find someone who understands that the commitment to accountability is more than simply the commitment to meet regularly. They must be willing to take time through the week to pray for you, call you, answer your calls, and check up on you. The calling to be a spiritual person who restores another caught in a sin is a high and holy calling that requires time.

True accountability also requires someone who possesses the biblical knowledge and practical wisdom to guide you toward purity. This does not require years of experience or advanced degrees. It can be any growing Christian who is walking in sexual purity and is willing to read this book along with you.

Finally, true accountability requires an effort to be committed in the long term. It's quite typical for these sorts of relationships to start strong, only to taper off after a relatively short period. When people get lazy and stop trying, failure is not far behind. Be sure your group is praying to be diligent over the long haul.

## You Need Grace to be Accountable

Accountability is an important biblical strategy in your fight for purity with the power of grace. Yet accountability is not productive in and of itself. Accountability must function properly if it's going to work. It's better to avoid driving than to drive a car with no brakes. In the same way, you can actually harm your pursuit of freedom if you don't ensure that your accountability is working as it should.

The right kind of accountability—characterized by initiative, openness, clean conversation, maturity, and serious answerability for sin—is hard. It takes more than guts to pursue it; it takes grace. Perhaps you have read this and are worried about entering this kind of relationship. If you are, confess to God that you're tempted to hide, seek the forgiving grace of Jesus, and then fight in prayer for the transforming grace to pursue real accountability. God knows your heart. He knows what you need, and he is eager to help you when you ask in faith.

# Fighting for Purity with the Power of Grace

1. Make a list of a few spiritually mature Christians you respect and would like to join you in accountability. Ideally, they should be believers from your local church or shared ministry who will encounter you in the normal course of life.

2. Make an appointment with your pastor, youth minister, community group leader, or some other Christian in spiritual authority over you. Talk to them about your struggle and ask if they would be willing to read this book with you, or if someone on your list may be a better choice. Also be willing to consider they may have a better suggestion you didn't consider.

3. Once you find a spiritually mature person who is willing to be an accountability partner, set up a regular time to meet every week or every other week. You should agree on an agenda for your time together. In the early stages it would be helpful to read and discuss one chapter of this book each week.

4. Pray and ask God to forgive you for any doubts, passivity, or hiding you see in your heart. Pray in faith for God to give you the grace to change and seek accountability.

# CHAPTER 4

# Using Radical Measures to Fight Pornography

I want to tell you the story of two guys who were totally hooked. But they weren't hooked on pornography; they were hooked on cookies. And these "guys" were not people at all; they were two fictional friends named Frog and Toad—the stars of a series of children's books I loved hearing as a kid and now love reading as a parent.

In my favorite story about Frog and Toad, Toad makes an amazing batch of cookies. He is so overwhelmed with how good they taste that he hops straight over to Frog's place to share the deliciousness. As the two devour these incredibly tasty cookies, they quickly realize they can't stop eating them. Just as they decide to have just one last cookie, they find they want to eat even more. Despite their resolve to quit eating, they find themselves continuing to indulge. Frog and Toad quickly realize that if they are ever going to stop eating cookies, they will have to do something to limit their access to them. The rest of the story details all the steps they take to make the cookies harder to get. Though you may be wondering what a children's story has to do with fighting for purity with the power of grace, hang on! This story contains a powerful lesson about defeating sin.

## Getting Serious in the Struggle against Sin

Many people struggle with pornography because *it is so easy for them to get* it. The simple truth is that if you keep pornography easily available, you will look at it sooner or later. If you want to experience true and lasting change, you can pray, beg, cry, and wail, but at the end of the day you will also need to be very practical. You will need to make porn less accessible. Jesus made this important point in the Sermon on the Mount:

> "You have heard that it was said, 'You shall not commit adultery.' But I tell you that anyone who looks at a woman lustfully has already committed adultery with her in his heart. If your right eye causes you to stumble, gouge it out and throw it away. It is better for you to lose one part of your body than for your whole body to be thrown into hell. And if your right hand causes you to stumble, cut it off and throw it away. It is better for you to lose one part of your body than for your whole body to go into hell."
>
> *Matthew 5:27–30*

Jesus speaks these words to people who are struggling with sexual sin. In other words, Jesus is speaking these words to *you*. He makes such a strong statement because he wants you to wake up to the seriousness of your sexual sin and to alert you to the radical measures necessary to deal with it.

Jesus calls Christians to a *serious standard* and a *serious strategy* because of the *serious stakes* involved.

First, Jesus provides a *serious standard*. If a person wants purity, it is not enough to avoid having a physical, sexual relationship with someone who is not his or her spouse. If they want purity, Jesus says, they must not *want* sex with someone who is not their spouse. Jesus raises the standard of purity from physical acts of fornication to lustful intentions of the heart and lustful looks of the eyes. He tells us we are adulterous people, not only when we have sex with someone who is not our spouse, but whenever we look at someone who is not our spouse and desire any sort of sexual relationship with that person. This truth highlights one of the many reasons that pornography is wrong: it reveals the evil, corrupt desires of our sinful heart.

Jesus follows this with a *serious strategy* for fighting sexual sin. If you are tempted to violate the standard and commit sexual sin, then Jesus says you must gouge out your eye or cut off your hand. You must not only remove these parts of your body; you must also throw them away. Jesus won't allow you to retain these sinning body parts in hopes of using them later. He commands that you cast them away and abandon any future prospect of using them again for sinful purposes.

To be clear, Jesus does not mean you must get an actual knife and literally remove these parts of your body. Jesus often speaks in powerful metaphors. After all, even people who lack eyes and hands can still lust and sin in their hearts. Jesus is urging something even *more* radical than a one-time physical amputation. He is telling us that when we are tempted to sin sexually, we must act aggressively—*every time* we are tempted and in *every way* required to avoid the sin. If you are struggling with pornography, Jesus wants you to understand that you will need to get tough with your sin. You will need to employ radical measures to limit your access and starve your temptation.

Finally, Jesus discusses the *serious stakes* of disobedience. Why does Jesus urge such radical measures? *Because of the life-and-death nature of the consequences.* Employing radical measures is the path to life, while indulging sin is the path to hell. God does not forbid sexual immorality because he wants you to be miserable; God forbids it because sexual immorality leads to brokenness, sadness, emptiness, death, and hell. Righteousness, on the other hand, leads to fullness, joy, peace, and life. According to Jesus, sin is not complicated. There are two simple choices and two guaranteed consequences—the easy path of sexual immorality, which will kill you, and the hard path of radical warfare against it, which will lead you to the fullness of life.

You may have already experienced a small taste of the hell that Jesus warns about for those who indulge in sexual immorality. If this is true for you, I want you to know it is possible for you to know the life that Jesus promises. You can have it—but it won't come at a discount. If you want the life God offers, you will have to get serious about resisting your sin. You will have to be aggressive. You will have to get radical. Amputation is not easy. It is extraordinarily painful and carries with it a sense of loss, but the reward is far better than the alternative.

You will need to employ radical measures in at least three areas. You look at porn when you have the *desire* to see it, when you have the *time* to look at it, and when it is *available* to you. Nobody looks at pornography without all three of these elements coming together. In your fight to be free from pornography, you must learn to take radical steps to eliminate each one.

## Radical Measures in Your Thought Life

Radical measures should begin in a critical area that is often overlooked—your thought life. This means looking more carefully at *how you think about pornography*. Are there specific times when you indulge in lustful fantasies? Are there places where you are particularly prone to think about pornography? The truth is that you could be all alone in a room filled with pornography and remain pure if you had no desire for it. In fact, this is the long-term goal. You will know you are finally free from pornography when you have full access to it and yet no desire for it. Though you're not there yet, that's where you're headed. And in order to get there, you will need to change the way you think about pornography.

Viewing pornography is typically the last stop on a long road of sexual sins. A dozen other things have gone wrong in your heart and mind by the time you actually look at porn. You will not have victory over pornography until you first have victory in the battles that come before you look. Foundationally, this battle begins in your heart—with your thinking. Imagine you have a garden with a flower that has ugly blossoms. You don't want to see the ugly bloom anymore. Every time the flower buds, you pluck it off. Predictably, the blossom keeps coming back. It will continue to do so until you remove the plant at the root. The same principle applies to the pornographic lust that is choking out good spiritual fruit in the garden of your heart. If you only attack the outward behavior, the problem will keep returning. You must uproot pornographic lust in your thinking, dealing with what Jesus unveils as the lustful intentions of your heart (Matthew 5:28).

I can guarantee failure if you wait to begin the fight against porn until you are alone in the dark with your computer. This is a battle that must be waged the very moment you become aware of your desire to see pornography. That very second is the time to take radical measures. And there are three radical measures you can take with regard to your thinking.

First, you must *repent immediately*. We talked about our need for repentance in the first chapter. Repentance isn't something that only takes place in tranquil moments of calm reflection or intense times of powerful resolve. Repentance is an ongoing practice, and it happens most commonly in the fog of temptation. Repentance is something you will do repeatedly in your long-term struggle against porn. In that initial moment of temptation, you must begin asking the Lord to forgive you for your lustful desires. You must ask him for grace to flee this temptation. You must plead with him to give you the power to do the other things I'll mention later in this chapter.

Second, you must *remember Scripture*. Scripture memory is not just a pious spiritual discipline for people who are more holy or mature than you are. Scripture memory is a powerful weapon that can give you victory in your battle against porn. The psalmist says to God, "I have hidden your word in my heart that I might not sin against you" (Psalm 119:11). The Bible—internalized as a treasure in your heart—is available as a powerful ally against temptation. You have access to an entire Bible full of passages you can hide in your heart to help you in temptation. You can memorize Psalm 119:11; Matthew 5:27–30; or any other Bible verse in this book. The passages you select do not even need to address sexual purity. A diverse stockpile of biblical truth is needed to combat the lies of temptation when they come.

Third, you must *reach out for help*. Repentance is crucial. Remembering the Bible is essential. But as important as it is to be armed with these powerful graces, you are not designed to fight the battles of sin and temptation alone. You must call in reinforcements. You should have several people you've talked with in advance who will hold you accountable, people you can call when you are in trouble. I often tell people that I want them to feel comfortable calling me at any time of the day or night. They might wake me up in the middle of the night, but it's better to do that than to sin. Reaching out to others *immediately* in the midst of temptation will often be difficult to do because sin loves the darkness and is skilled at presenting attractive excuses. You must fight these temptations and expose the darkness to the light.

## Radical Measures in Your Use of Time

In addition to a transformation in your thinking, the second area in which you must take extreme measures is your use of time. A person who desires pornography can only view it when it's available and when they have time alone to view it. Imagine you have a desire to see pornography and are in a room surrounded by porn. If one of your pastors or an accountability partner happens to be in the room with you, you would probably be able to resist looking—despite your desire and the availability of the porn. Now, take those people away and you're instantly tempted again. Why? Because now you're *alone.*

This means you must limit the time you spend alone—especially in the early phases of the struggle against pornography. Be honest with your accountability partner about the typical times when you are alone and find yourself tempted. Make plans to spend those times with others. You can study together, take a walk, play sports, read the Bible and pray, or watch a movie. You can even have an accountability partner scheduled to call you during those times (with the requirement that you must pick up the phone) to check in on you. If you're married, you may need to commit to going to bed at the same time as your spouse, even if you don't feel tired. Cut back as much as possible on the times when you are alone and tempted to indulge in pornography.

## Radical Measures for Cutting Off Access to Pornography

If you are serious about being free from pornography, then you will also need to employ radical measures that affect how you access pornography. Often, this is the area most people think about first when they are considering radical measures, but they may not go far enough for the changes to be effective. Because of this, I will offer some practical and thorough advice for severing yourself from your sources of pornography.

You most likely view porn from the same sources again and again. You must eliminate, not limit, your access to these outlets for pornography. There are three main ways in which a person can access pornography today: pay for it in a store, view it on the Internet or TV, or access it through a friend. We will talk about radical measures for each one. Since our sin turns us into inventors of evil (see Romans 1:30), you may find other creative avenues for accessing porn, especially as technological advances make it even more accessible. If so, be diligent to apply the principles below to these new sources as well.

Let's say you obtained pornography by buying it at a pornographic video store or renting it from a movie rental location. If so, you must take radical measures to make your access to these places as difficult as possible.

First, take radical measures to restrict your ability to view any movies you might purchase. This means you hand over to your accountability partner any devices that play movies—DVD players, televisions, computers, and the like. You also need to destroy any movies, magazines, or pictures you already possess.

Second, take radical measures to restrict your ability to keep porn where you live. You should give your accountability partner total access to your home, which should include keys and your explicit permission and encouragement to enter at any point to do a spot-check of your residence and your car. Your accountability partner should have permission to come when you're not there and examine even the most private areas. If you live alone, you should consider getting a roommate to make it even more challenging to keep immoral material around.

Third, you may need to take radical measures that restrict your ability to travel freely. If you have access to pornography in stores because you have freedom to travel anywhere you want, you may need to limit this kind of unmonitored mobility. There are a few ways you can limit yourself. Many smartphones have the capability for GPS tracking. You can install such software on your phone so the person helping you can check where you are (or where you've been). You will think twice about visiting a place you shouldn't if you know your accountability partner can tell you were there. It also may be necessary for you to forfeit your freedom to drive a car for a season. This sacrifice won't end your life, but it will require some adjustments. You may need to arrange for your accountability partner to hold your keys until you need them for a specific reason. You would then turn the keys in as soon as you finished your obligation. Depending on your situation, you could bike to work, take the bus, join a carpool, or have a family member or church friend drive you. You might even need to find a new job or a different place to live so you can put your driving on hold indefinitely. The point is that you cannot maintain the unbridled mobility you currently have to access pornography whenever temptation strikes.

Fourth, take radical measures to restrict your purchasing ability. If you buy your porn (either at a store or electronically), it is entirely possible you need to give up some of your freedom to spend your own money. You may need to provide your bank passwords to someone who can monitor your transactions. If you do, you should agree to avoid cash withdrawals or to provide receipts for any cash purchases. You should also commit to providing receipts for any purchases at places like grocery, drug, and convenience stores where cash withdrawals can be added to purchases and won't show up on statements. You can arrange to receive a daily or weekly allowance from your accountability partner or spouse. Even then, it would be necessary to account for the allowance at the end of the time period with receipts.

Perhaps you obtain pornography by viewing it on the Internet or television. Three radical measures can help you limit your access to pornography from these sources. First, you can ask someone to put passwords on your computer, phone, or TV that will make it impossible for you to access the Internet or to view pornographic material without the code, which only your accountability partner or perhaps your spouse would know. You also should be denied administrative privileges on any devices that allow this. Such access should be reserved for the person who is holding you accountable.

Second, install accountability software on your computer and phone. This software is inexpensive, is available from many different sources, and either blocks objectionable websites or records your Internet activity and sends it to someone of your choosing. It's best to use software that does both. You also should implement filtering and monitoring strategies for your router—not just for your individual devices.

Third, you can get rid of any equipment you use to view pornography. In our high-tech age we often consider it impossible to exist without our computers, tablet devices, smartphones, or TVs. The honest truth is that you don't *need* any electronic device, but you do need to be holy. The inconvenience will be worth the gain in holiness.

Doing all of these things can be a particular challenge when traveling out of town. When traveling on business, you will need to be especially diligent in using each of these measures. In addition to the things mentioned here, you may need to agree to show your accountability partner an itemized hotel bill to help you avoid the purchase of any movies in your room. Because many hotel televisions make immoral programming available without an additional fee, it may be necessary to have a maintenance worker remove the television from your room. They really will do this if you ask them. One man I counseled would text me a time-stamped picture of the television being removed from his room whenever he was out on the road.

Finally, you may be getting your pornography from someone else who has it. Perhaps you have a roommate, parent, sibling, neighbor, coworker, or friend who has a stash of material you can look at whenever you wish. You might be using someone else's computer or phone to look at pornography without their knowledge. If so, the most effective radical measure is to confess your struggle to them and ask them to remove the opportunity for you to view it when you're around. Such an admission may be painful or even embarrassing, but keep in mind that it's better than cutting off your hand! And according to Jesus, both of these are far less painful than hell. Just because something is hard doesn't mean you shouldn't do it. Pray for the grace of a changed heart, and then obey by doing the right thing, regardless of the cost.

One word of caution here. Before you talk with the person who is intentionally or unintentionally giving you access to porn, you should inform your accountability partner. There may be some situations where it's unwise and even dangerous to approach a person who (knowingly or unknowingly) provides you with access to pornography. Before you get involved in a relationally complex and personally risky situation, you should ask a trusted outside source for wisdom.

## Are You Ready to Get Serious?

I realize that after reading this, some of you are freaking out. Reading about these radical measures raises all sorts of objections: *What will I do without my smartphone? How will I text ... get sports scores ... update social media? What will I do without my car? How can I live without my debit card? How can I tell my parents what I've been doing on the computer? Is this guy serious?* Believe me, I've heard them all. If you are stressing about these things, it's because you are considering the seriousness of the strategy without considering the seriousness of the stakes. Let's not forget that Jesus commands amputation because he is concerned that we avoid hell and pursue life in him. Do you fully grasp the serious consequences of your sin? Indulging in pornography is like drinking spiritual poison. If you do nothing, it will kill you sooner or later. Get a clear picture of what pornography is doing to your heart, your mind, and your life. When you do, you will want to get serious and do anything you can to stop the spread, regardless of how radical it might seem.

Thankfully, not everyone will have to employ all of these measures, but everyone will have to employ some of them. Talk honestly with the person helping you and make wise decisions together about which measures to take. These measures aren't meant to be convenient; they're meant to be radical, difficult, painful, and costly. No one removes a limb because it's fun or handy. They do it because they realize they cannot keep the limb and live. It's a life-and-death decision.

## Frog, Toad, and Radical Measures

Frog and Toad knew they had to take steps to get far away from the cookies Frog had made. They tried a number of things—putting the cookies in a box, tying up the box, and putting the box on a very high shelf. Our amphibious friends quickly realized, however, that they could always undo the measures they put in place. They could still get the cookies if they really tried. So at the end of the story they take the most radical step of all and throw the cookies to the birds. Now, with no more cookies to eat, Toad decides to go home—and bake a cake.

The story of Frog and Toad teaches a critically important truth in fighting temptation: *outward measures, regardless of how radical they are, can never change your heart.* This is why it is critical to employ radical measures in your thought life first. You need more than a change in your circumstances to win the battle; you need a change in your heart. Frog and Toad tried putting the cookies far out of reach, but eventually they found a way to eat them, because no matter what they tried, they still *wanted* to eat the cookies. Never forget this lesson. You can try to remove porn's availability. You can eliminate your time alone. Yet you will still seek out porn if you desire it. This is why Jesus and the good news of the gospel is the only sure hope for those who want to be free from porn. Only Jesus has the power to change your heart desires, and he does this as you believe in his forgiving and transforming grace.

This emphasis on the need for change in your heart does not mean ignoring other, more outward forms of radical action. Taking steps to limit your time and remove the source of temptation just need to be put in their proper place.

Outward radical measures do not change your desires, but they are necessary for two crucial reasons.

First, radical measures give you space in which to grow. Change takes time. Old ways of living must die; new ways of living must form. New kinds of thinking must be learned. If you are enslaved to pornography, God will not usually change your desires instantly but by degrees (see 2 Corinthians 3:18). Radical measures allow the space and time needed for you to direct your attention toward Christ instead of porn.

Second, employing radical measures gives you an opportunity to "produce fruit in keeping with repentance" (Matthew 3:8). As you learn to rely on God's help to set you free, you will want the full-blown power of having new desires. As you press forward in growth, you can still experience some change before your new desires have fully formed. These external measures are the first steps of change, and even though they don't automatically transform your internal desires, they are expressions of *real* change. You need the grace of Jesus to accomplish them. When you experience his grace to take these first, hard, faltering steps, you are seeing the fruit of God's work. Seeing this fruit helps give you confidence that Jesus will also give you the grace to experience the fullness of change that you are seeking.

This wonderful and progressive change is given to you by Jesus through his forgiving and transforming grace. As you continue to fight for purity with the power of grace, you must continue to seek God's forgiveness and his power to be different. Cry out to Jesus. Remember his death on the cross and how it purchases your forgiveness and your obedience. Believe that Jesus' blood pays for any sinful lack of seriousness and gives you power to employ every radical measure necessary.

# Fighting for Purity with the Power of Grace

1. Consider your need to employ radical measures in your thinking. Make a commitment to repent the moment your thoughts begin to drift toward impurity. Ask Jesus for help to follow through with this commitment. Make a plan with your accountability partner to hold you accountable. Think through an initial passage of Scripture you can begin using to fight temptation in your heart. Write it down and begin memorizing it. Finally, make a plan with your accountability partner to commit to call for help when you are tempted.

2. Consider your need to employ radical measures in your use of time. Write down and discuss with your accountability partner the times when you are most tempted to view porn. Make a plan together to fill this time with activities that will move you toward purity.

3. Identify, write down, and share with your accountability partner the places where you access pornography. Do you get it online and on TV, purchase it from a store, or get it from someone you know? Review this chapter and write down all the radical measures you will take to block your access to the sources.

4. When taking these steps seems too hard or when you find yourself facing temptation, meet with Jesus. Ask him for his help, believing he will give it to you.

# CHAPTER 5

# Using Confession to Fight Pornography

Tom was frustrated. He sat in the office with me and another pastor as we confronted him with our suspicions that he had been looking at pornography. Tom admitted that he had spent a considerable amount of time looking at porn, but he stressed that he had quit almost a week ago. He knew what he had done was wrong, so he told another friend at church and downloaded accountability software onto his computer.

We were encouraged by these steps, but then we asked Tom if he had confessed this sin to his wife. He had not. When we insisted he must tell his wife what he had done, Tom became deeply agitated. In frustration he protested, "My wife doesn't know. Telling her about this would *create* a conflict rather than solve one. And there's really nothing to tell her since I haven't looked in a while." Finally he added, "It's not like I committed adultery with an actual person. I never stopped having sex with my wife." Tom strongly felt that confessing his sin to his wife was a bad idea.

Eventually, after talking it over, Tom agreed to confess his sin to his wife. He did what we encouraged him to do, and in the end their relationship was stronger for it. Tom later told me that confessing his sin to his wife was one of the main things the Lord used to keep him from ever returning to pornography.

Before Tom was willing to confess to his wife, we had to prove to him that confessing to her would actually help him in his battle against sin. In the first chapter, I talked about the importance of confessing our sin to God; in this chapter, we'll be looking at the need to confess our sin to others. My prayer is that, like Tom, you will understand the powerful grace of confessing your sin to those who are harmed by your involvement with pornography.

## The Importance of Confession

Tom needed to know our advice was biblical before he would accept it, and I'm sure the same is true for you. The Bible states, "Whoever conceals their sins does not prosper, but the one who confesses and renounces them finds mercy" (Proverbs 28:13). At least three truths in this passage illustrate how important it is for you to be a person who confesses sin.

First, it is important to confess sin because the Bible tells us that confession is the way we receive the promise of God's mercy and blessing. This proverb teaches us that it is bad to cover up our sins and that it is good to confess them openly. Notice this is not in the form of a command—it's a promise. The Bible promises that there is no prosperity for those who cover up their sin. On the other hand, good things will come to those who expose their evil deeds. God's Word graciously calls us to confess our sins because confessing is better than concealing. Like surgery, pain actually promotes healing. So the first and most obvious reason you should expose your sin of looking at pornography is that it is a mark of wisdom to seek the merciful blessings that come with uncovering sin.

A second reason it is important to confess sin has to do with the *kinds* of mercy that come to those who confess. One kind of mercy that comes with confession is the blessing of openness and restoration in relationship. Sin separates you from those you've sinned against, creating walls between you and those you love. How can you repair this brokenness? What can you do to restore what your sin has destroyed? In the Bible there are no take backs, do-overs, or repeats. Sin is not a misstep corrected by simple adjustments. It is only through a process of confessing our sin that God allows us to make right what has been damaged and broken. To be restored to those you love—to receive mercy—you must first confess your sin.

Tom sinned against people who didn't know they had been sinned against. Tom's wife may not have been aware of his sin, but her lack of knowledge doesn't change the fact that what Tom did broke his commitment to remain faithful to his wife. Regardless of whether Tom's wife knew it or not, his sin led to a lack of openness and sincerity in their relationship. Tom could keep his wife in the dark, living in ignorance, but it is far better to desire a relationship with his wife built on honesty, trust, and full awareness of the other's strengths and struggles. The only way for Tom to receive this mercy—the only way for *you* to receive this mercy—is to confess your hidden sin.

A third reason it is important to confess your sin relates to yet another kind of mercy that accompanies confession. James tells us that "God opposes the proud but shows favor to the humble" (James 4:6). There are two important implications of this verse that relate to the struggle with pornography. On the one hand, I will assume you want to experience God's merciful favor as you seek to move toward purity. After all, you may well be reading a book like this because you are desperate to know God's power.

On the other hand, most people don't want to confess their sin because of embarrassment or fear. You might be embarrassed about your struggle, not wanting others to know. You may be afraid of how they will respond when they discover what you have done. You can even make these fears sound holy and loving and turn them into legitimate reasons to avoid confession: *I don't want to put my loved one through a difficult ordeal. It would be wrong of me to inflict my troubles on those around me. Telling my spouse will just make matters worse. I can change my life privately without them needing to know.* But at the heart of it, there is likely a more selfish reason for not confessing your secret sin: you are loving yourself and your reputation more than you love God and others; you are proud.

So how does a proud person come to know God's favor? How does a person full of self-love receive God's mercy to change? In James 4:6, God speaks his promise to you: *If you want my favor, humble yourself; if you want my mercy, confess your sin.* There is no mercy or favor for those who arrogantly cover their sin and keep it hidden. You will find God's grace to change only when you humbly confess your sin—not just to God, but to all those you have wronged, whether they know it or not.

# A Framework for Confessing Your Sin

Hopefully, I've convinced you that confession is the path to healing and blessing. But I need to warn you as well. You need to be careful. Confessing your sin can be a tricky business. We live in a culture that does not understand how to confess sin. There are many common and hurtful mistakes people tend to make. Because your sin may come as a painful shock to those you have sinned against, it is very important to consider beforehand how to confess your sin in the wisest way possible. Here are six critical guidelines to make your confession as helpful as it should be.

## 1. Confess Your Sin to All Who Have Been Touched by Your Sin.

The Bible has much to say about confessing sin, and we can't look at all of it here. But if I were to try to boil dozens of verses down to one principle, I would say that the circle of your confession should be as broad as the circle of your sin. If you draw a circle around all the people your sin touches, then you should confess to everyone in that circle. God stands in the center of the circle, since all sin is ultimately committed against him (Psalm 51:4), but there are usually plenty of other people in the circle as well. You should confess to your spouse, since indulging in pornography is a blatant violation of the sexual fidelity promised in your marriage vows. You should confess to your fiancée for a similar reason—you're preemptively breaking the vows you are committing to make. You will need to confess to accountability partners, since viewing porn is a break in your relationship with these fellow believers who have partnered with you for spiritual growth.

You will need to confess to anyone whose equipment, money, or space you used—if you used your neighbor's computer, your friend's money, or your hallmate's room, you should confess to them. There will often be others in the circle of your sin as well. The point is that you must confess to everyone you have wronged, even if they are unaware.

## 2. Do Not Confess Your Sin to Those Who Are Not Touched by Your Sin.

Given the first point, you might think it is safe to assume this guideline. It isn't. Sometimes our guilt over sin can lead us to confession that is unwise or includes too many people out of a misplaced desire to "come clean" and "be real." Here's a story that illustrates how damaging this can be.

Several years ago, a male student of mine asked to speak privately with his female friend at the school. During that conversation this young man confessed that he had been plagued with lust for this young woman. He knew it was wrong to have lustful fantasies about her filling his mind, and so he asked for her forgiveness. I cannot express how much this young woman was freaked out by this conversation. I found out about it as she sat in my office crying, wondering how in the world she should respond.

What is wrong with this confession? After all, the young man was well-meaning, and he wanted to be serious about exposing the darkness in his heart to the light. It must have taken extreme humility and courage to share such a sin with a young woman he did not know well. His problem was that his method unwisely included more people than necessary. This man's desire to unburden himself was tainted with his own selfishness. He wasn't thinking about how troubling this information would be for this young woman, who had no idea there was any problem. The problem with his confession was not that the woman was unaware of the sin; it was the fact that the lustful man's sin had not directly impacted her. Lust is first a sin of the heart and a sin against God. This man had not expressed his lustful thoughts in a way that affected this young woman. The guilty man needed to make the sin a matter of confession to God alone.

The lesson to learn from this is that you must not think of confession as being exclusively for you; you must also see it as an effort to serve God and neighbor that is guided by the teaching of Scripture and not by your own desires. Be sure the people to whom you confess your sins are within the circle of those offended by your sin. This principle does not mean it is always wrong to talk with others about your sin struggles in general terms as a testimony to God's faithful care in your life. It also doesn't mean you exclude spiritual mentors who can help hold you accountable for your thoughts and temptations. It does mean you need to be careful about involving people in your struggles against sin. As you consider these first two principles, you will likely have many questions about whom to include in your confession. If you do, pray. Ask God for wisdom. Seek the wisdom of others, such as a pastor, a wise Christian friend, a parent, or another wise believer. Ask for help as you sort these things out.

## 3. Confess Your Sin with a Willingness to Accept the Consequences of Your Sin.

Tom's marriage was ultimately stronger because of his honesty about his sin, but there were still bumps along the way. When Tom initially confessed, his wife was hurt, shocked, and angry. She cried. She asked how he could do this. She charged that he must not think she was attractive. She made him sleep on the couch. Tom responded by expressing his own frustration to his wife. "But I did the right thing! I confessed! And now you're angry with me? Shouldn't you be more gracious? More willing to forgive?"

The truth was that his wife *was* willing to forgive, but she needed time to process the crushing news Tom had delivered. Tom was frustrated because his expectations were unrealistic. He should have expected his wife to be wounded by his confession. He should have expected relational consequences. It was naive and unfair for him to assume his confession would be a quick fix. Instead, he needed to understand that his confession was the *first step* toward a solution.

When you confess your sin, you need to expect that those you've wronged are likely to be upset, angry, and deeply hurt by your sin. You should expect relational consequences, not all of which will be in just proportion to what you have done. Remember that we always sin against other sinners. Offering forgiveness can be just as hard as confessing sin.

The people we sin against know how to sin in response. A loved one may respond with emotional shock. Instead of reacting to their reaction, be prepared to stay calm and give them time for your confession to settle in. If a parent reacts with sinful anger, trust God! Instead of blaming them for their response and dulling your confession with an accusation, put yourself in their shoes. View their shock, hurt, and anger as another reflection of the seriousness of your sin and the deep wounds it has left in the hearts of those you love. No matter what the response, trust God to give you the grace to know how to handle it. Talk to the wise person helping you, and figure out what to do together. After you resolve to confess, know that it's not your job to figure out all the possibilities, plan for every contingency, and worry about all the potential responses. Your job is simply to be faithful and do the next right thing. Confess with a willingness to accept consequences and work toward long-term restoration.

## 4. Consider Confessing Your Sin with a Third Party Who Can Help with the Response.

When Tom agreed that he should confess his sin, we offered to be present with him or to let him do it alone. Tom asked us to go with him. In fact, in my years in ministry I've never had a man in Tom's situation tell me he wanted to confess his sin alone. I think choosing to confess with a third party present is often a very wise decision.

When you confess a serious and secret sin like pornography to someone you love, you will deal with countless variables. Having a trusted person there helps you handle those variables. When someone else is present, it can keep you from chickening out and not confessing. They can help you provide the right amount of detail so you avoid saying too much or not enough. They can guide you in knowing how to answer questions the other person asks and can be an encouragement to your loved one that you really are seeking outside help and not handling things by yourself. Having a third party present also encourages the other person to avoid a sinful response. Finally, a wise third party can help chart a path forward so both people know what to do after the confession.

When you select the person who accompanies you, it is wise to choose a mature Christian whom the other person can respect and trust. An accountability partner isn't necessarily the best choice. You might feel comfortable going with this person, but he or she might not be the best choice to inspire confidence and comfort with the person you're addressing. Talk it over, pray for wisdom, and make a thoughtful decision that will serve the process and the best interests of the person to whom you are confessing.

## 5. Confess Your Sin Thoroughly, but Not Necessarily Exhaustively.

In her pain, Tom's wife demanded to know the specifics of what Tom had been viewing. She asked detailed questions about what the women he was watching looked like, and what they were doing. Such questions put Tom in an awkward position. He wanted to be honest with his wife and not anger her by refusing the information, but he wasn't sure it was helpful for her to know such details. Tom was entirely right to have these qualms. In my experience, many spouses (especially wives) hunt for meticulous details in the aftermath of such devastating revelations. When they find that their spouses have been living in a repeated pattern of secret sin, they want unfiltered access to every bit of information. They want to gain a sense of control by obtaining information they have been denied. Such impulses are understandable, but usually not helpful. Providing graphic details about the kind of porn you have been viewing can actually harm the restoration process. Vivid details, once lodged in the mind, are hard to extract. A person may feel that knowing such particulars will help, but it actually hurts.

At the same time, it was important for Tom—and for you as well—to be forthright and thorough in his confession. Those to whom you confess need to know you have a problem with pornography (not just a struggle with lust), and they need some idea of how serious the struggle is. They may need to know how frequent the struggle is—every day, every week, every month? They may need to know if you are in financial or legal trouble. They may need to know if you are looking at a type of porn that indicates you have other problems besides a desire to view heterosexual pornography. Talk with your accountability partner about how to confess the details as thoroughly as possible while knowing that the person hearing your confession absolutely does not need to know exhaustive details about what you have looked at.

Putting a cap on the amount of information you provide can be tricky to do. The person you are confessing to may view your restraint as a sign that you are being evasive and less than forthcoming. This is another reason you should consider having a third party with you who can gently help the other person realize the prudence of a controlled confession.

## 6. Confess Your Sin without Making Any Excuses for Your Sin.

Tom made a critical error when he confessed to his wife. After he fessed up, Tom said something foolish before either of us in the room could stop him. He commented that perhaps if she had a more active sexual relationship with him, he would not have been tempted. His wife did not take that very well.

Her response was understandable because Tom's suggestion was selfish and wrong. This kind of statement transfers the responsibility for your sin onto another person. When you sin, *you* are the one responsible (Mark 7:21–23). Other people can sin against you, make your life difficult, and entice you to sin, but they can never *make* you sin. When you sin, it is always your fault, and you should never say or do anything to make it sound like the fault lies elsewhere. If someone did sin against you, it is necessary to bring that up only after you have confessed and taken full responsibility for your own sin (Matthew 7:1–5).

## Confession and Fear

I know I'm asking you to do something that is hard. As you consider taking this step toward purity, it may feel like confessing a secret sin is one of the hardest things you have ever been asked to do. I know how overwhelming it can feel to consider confessing such a serious sin and to be terrified that those you love will hate you for it. To overcome this fear, you must focus on two truths.

First, you must avoid living in fear and instead trust in God's Word. As you confront the challenge of confessing your sin to others, you have a choice to make. Will you follow your fears and stay silent, or will you live by faith and confess? From your perspective, there will be many reasons to remain silent. You will think about preserving your shell of integrity, protecting your loved ones from harm, or sparing your relationships pain and heartache. God's Word pierces through these confused, fearful, and selfish arguments with a bold and clear message: *He who conceals his sins does not prosper, but whoever confesses and renounces them finds mercy.* Will you trust your twisted wisdom or God's trustworthy Word? Will you find mercy, or will you know distress?

Second, if you are to fight your fears and know the mercy of confession, you will find you can't do it yourself. You need power. You need grace. The confession we have discussed in this chapter must be covered in grace at the beginning of the process and at the end. We have already talked about the mercy and grace that comes to those who confess their sin. Here we must acknowledge that in order to experience the grace that flows from confession of sin, you need the power that leads to confession. The power you need that leads to your confession of sin is the forgiving and transforming grace we have discussed from the outset of this book. You need to seek God's forgiving grace for not confessing your sin, and you need God's transforming grace to empower you to make your confession. When you receive God's grace to make your confession to others, then you will receive God's grace, which flows from that confession. Confession is bookended with grace. If you are tempted to follow your fears, confess those fears to Jesus. Ask him for his forgiving grace. Beseech God to give you his transforming grace that will empower you to confess your sin where it is essential to do so. Jesus loves you. He wants you to be pure. If you trust him, he will meet you with kindness and give you what you need to be forgiven … and to change.

# Fighting for Purity with the Power of Grace

1. Who are the people your sin has affected that you need to approach with an honest confession? Do you have a spouse or fiancée? Have you lied to those you love so you could indulge in pornography? Have you used the technology or money of people who would not approve? Write down the people in the circle of your sin.

2. Perhaps there are people you are unsure about. As you think about confessing your sin to all who are touched by your sin — and not confessing to those who are not — there may be some gray areas. Write down the names of people you have questions about. Talk with the person helping you about these concerns.

3. Do you have any questions for your accountability partner about your confession? Are there others whom it would be wise to take with you as you confess your sin? Write down any names and discuss them with your accountability partner.

4. Now you need to encounter God's forgiving and transforming grace. Where have you been guilty of sin in the midst of the call to confess your sin? Have you avoided confession, even though you knew it was necessary? What fears have you believed instead of God's Word? Write them down and pray through the list, asking for the forgiving grace of Jesus. Now ask Jesus to empower you to be obedient to confess your sin.

5. Make an appointment within twenty-four hours with the first person on your list of those who need to hear your confession. Move through your list in a faithful and timely way, working with your accountability partner on any issues that arise.

# CHAPTER 6

# Using Your Spouse (or Your Singleness) to Fight Pornography

The first car I ever owned was a 1987 Oldsmobile Cutlass Ciera. You might not think that sounds like a very cool car, but that's because you never saw it. If you'd seen it, you would be *positive* it was not a cool car. It was boxy and gray. It made a not-so-stylish whistling noise that didn't help my reputation in high school. The noise and the boxy, gray exterior was just the beginning, though. When you actually squeaked open a door, you saw the hyper-uncool burgundy seats made of Naugahyde. If you don't know what Naugahyde is, then you are uncommonly blessed. It's a fabric that they coat in plastic so it resembles leather. Eventually it cracks, pinches your skin, and even sticks to you. I was thankful for my car, but it was not a great car. In fact, now that I think about it, I really don't want to think about my old Olds anymore.

I'd like to stop thinking about the unpleasantness of whistling Oldsmobiles and cracked Naugahyde digging into my thighs. However, it's hard to get the image out of my mind. What should I do? I could try really hard *not* to think about the car. I could try thinking to myself, *I need to stop thinking about that Oldsmobile. That Cutlass brings back bad memories of expensive repairs and classmates' jokes made at my expense—memories I would like to get out of my mind. That car was a rolling junkyard, so I need to quit dwelling on it.*

Do you notice something about my effort to quit thinking about my old gray car? It isn't working. Even though I'm trying really hard to quit thinking about that unpleasant automobile, my efforts are ineffective. Every thought that goes through my mind—though motivated by a desire to quit thinking about the car—only presses the image of it deeper into my mind. I need another strategy.

My problem is that I am focusing on the very thing I want to stop thinking about. Instead, I need to start thinking about something else—something different. Let me tell you about the car I drive now. It's a Toyota Camry. I admit it's still not the coolest car on the market today, but I can't help liking it. The air-conditioning actually works. The engine runs so quietly that I literally cannot hear it. At times I've turned the key twice, assuming the car wasn't on because I couldn't hear anything rattling. It has a CD player, cloth seats, automatic windows, and cruise control. I may not be hip, but I don't care. I am thankful for my Camry.

Did you notice what just happened? I had to stop thinking about my old car in order to begin thinking about my new car. Focusing on my Camry is more effective in changing my thinking than trying *not* to think about my old Cutlass Ciera.

This illustrates a very powerful principle: *You can never stop thinking about something by trying not to think about it.* If you want to get something out of your mind, you must begin thinking about something else.

The Bible tells us this is a vital principle for how we change. We must refocus our thinking away from porn and toward something holy. God wants to change our thinking, not by having us focus on the things we're trying to quit thinking about, but by replacing old, sinful thoughts with new, righteous thoughts.

So what does all of this have to do with the title of this chapter—the idea that you can, and should, use your spouse (or if you are single, your singleness) to fight pornography? A key passage of Scripture—Proverbs 5—powerfully expresses this principle of redirected thinking and calls you away from the impurity of sexual immorality and toward the purity of a sexual relationship with your spouse. We will look at the entire chapter in two sections. Here is how the first section reads:

> My son, pay attention to my wisdom,
>> turn your ear to my words of insight,
> that you may maintain discretion
>> and your lips may preserve knowledge.
> For the lips of the adulterous woman drip honey,
>> and her speech is smoother than oil;
> but in the end she is bitter as gall,
>> sharp as a double-edged sword.
> Her feet go down to death;
>> her steps lead straight to the grave.
> She gives no thought to the way of life;
>> her paths wander aimlessly, but she does not know it.
> Now then, my sons, listen to me;
>> do not turn aside from what I say.

Keep to a path far from her,
> do not go near the door of her house,
lest you lose your honor to others
> and your dignity to one who is cruel,
lest strangers feast on your wealth
> and your toil enrich the house of another.
At the end of your life you will groan,
> when your flesh and body are spent.
You will say, "How I hated discipline!
> How my heart spurned correction!
I would not obey my teachers
> or turn my ear to my instructors.
And I was soon in serious trouble
> in the assembly of God's people."

*Proverbs 5:1–14*

If you are looking for the word *pornography*, you will not find it in Proverbs 5. Although there wasn't anything like our modern idea of pornography when Proverbs 5 was written, the adulterous woman mentioned there can be taken to include any sexually immoral woman—whether encountered through porn or in any situation in life. With this in mind, Proverbs 5 is one of the most honest statements about pornography you will ever read.

## From Temptation to Threat: The Forbidden Woman

Proverbs 5 directs our attention in ways that keep our thoughts moving forward. King Solomon, who had lived a lust-fueled life himself, begins with an honest statement about the powerful temptations of the forbidden woman. The text reads, "The lips of the adulterous woman drip honey, and her speech is smoother than oil." The Bible is honest in stating that there is a sinister appeal about this woman who promises sexual pleasure without the commitment and investment of a marital relationship. God clearly does not approve of this attraction, as elsewhere in Scripture he calls people to sexual faithfulness and fidelity in marriage. But Solomon knows full well that the temptations are present—and pervasive.

Proverbs 5 does not stop there, however. The passage keeps our minds moving, showing us the temptations of the forbidden woman. Solomon goes on to unpack how dangerously threatening she is. He reveals the jagged truth about the forbidden woman and the frightening truth about the man who is drawn to her. First, he tells us this woman is dangerous and deadly: "In the end she is bitter as gall, sharp as a double-edged sword. Her feet go down to death; her steps lead straight to the grave." Through the words of Solomon, God shows us the appalling substance beneath the appealing surface. Porn is only appealing when you remain at the surface level of your attraction and fail to see the consequences. Your thinking stops at the tempting lips of honey, the speech as smooth as oil, and you fail to think about what comes next. God wants to move your thinking forward—to what follows the perverse "sweetness" of temptation. The very next verse reveals the painful death behind the misleading mask. The truth about the forbidden woman of porn is that she is not as sweet and smooth as she first appears. She is bitter and sharp, and those who follow her are led to a place of death. The sinful logic of porn only works if you don't think about it very hard.

God also makes it clear that the forbidden woman herself is deceived: "She gives no thought to the way of life; her paths wander aimlessly, but she does not know it." Women acting in pornography are dangerous because they will lead you away from the path of life, but have you ever considered that they are deceived and themselves led astray? The woman your eyes selfishly consume doesn't think about the way of life; she wanders aimlessly and ignorantly. The truth is that women involved in the porn industry really need men who will spend energy pointing them to Christ and helping them experience freedom from their slavery to sin, not men who use them for selfish and perverse pleasures. In the end, you should be broken over porn, not just because it damages your relationships with God and others, but because you are using women to serve your sinful flesh instead of sharing Christ with them.

Solomon points to truth about the adulterous woman, but he also reveals truth about the consequences of sexual sin. God shows us that when a man goes near the forbidden woman, he faces horrible consequences in *three* areas: he gives his honor and years to the merciless; he gives his strength and labors to strangers; and his flesh and body are consumed. To put it simply, pornography destroys your time, your strength, and ultimately your body. If you're unconvinced, listen to the story of a man I know named Jamie.

Jamie grew up in a nominally Christian, conservative home. When he left for college, he was what most would consider a good kid—responsible and hardworking. Jamie wasn't at college for long before he became involved with a group of young men who introduced him to pornography. Jamie loved it. He had never seen a naked woman before and had certainly never seen sex. Jamie loved porn because it allowed him to enjoy women who, he believed, were prettier than anyone he could ever have a relationship with in real life, all without any fear of rejection.

Porn was so easy and so fun that Jamie couldn't get enough of it. At first he was shy about walking into a store to buy it, but he quickly got over his initial embarrassment. Eventually he placed a huge bookcase in his living room full of nothing but pornographic videos. Any shame he once had about using pornography was now gone.

Several years later, Jamie met Alyssa. They enjoyed spending time together and started a serious relationship that quickly became sexual. Alyssa knew about Jamie's porn and didn't like it, but she assumed porn was just a normal thing for guys. She was a bit uncomfortable when Jamie began asking her to watch pornography with him, but she wanted to make him happy, and so she forced herself to get used to it.

Jamie and Alyssa eventually got married. After their wedding, Alyssa was shocked at how quickly Jamie lost interest in her. Their times of sexual intimacy were rare and never happened without the use of pornography. After a few years of this, Alyssa became disgusted. Jamie's porn collection had grown so large that it now took up almost the entire basement. He would return home from work and descend into the basement to indulge in porn late into the night. He was often late for work because he had no strength to get out of bed after late nights watching actors fornicate on screen.

Alyssa wanted out of the marriage. By now, however, she had given birth to twin daughters and was worried about how she could raise a family by herself. She tried fighting for her marriage to no avail. Jamie had moved a bed into the basement and would hardly speak to her. He lost his job and spent all of his time in the basement instead of looking for employment. One afternoon Jamie came upstairs and asked one of his daughters to come into the basement and play. Alyssa took the girls and left.

Jamie is now in his sixties. He doesn't have a job and lives with his elderly father. All he does, day after day, is look at porn. He doesn't care about work, his ex-wife, or his grown daughters. He is a miserable sight to see. He is unshaven, has missing teeth, smells bad, and wears dirty clothes. Talking to him is nearly impossible, as it seems he doesn't even know how to have a relationship with a real person anymore.

Jamie's story is a bad one. In fact, you might read this and feel pretty good right now, congratulating yourself that you're not nearly as bad as he is. You might also be thinking you would never let your problem get so extreme. If so, you are missing the entire point of Proverbs 5.

In his Word, God is warning you to stay away from the forbidden woman because of the devastating consequences she brings. Though the initial stages of temptation seem innocent, fun, and even enjoyable, eventually the sin of indulging in the adulterous woman of porn will take over your life and consume your time, your strength, and your body. When you turn to her, you lose the freedom and opportunity to determine the consequences. That's the warning God gives to us in his Word—even though you may not see the death and destruction that pornography brings today, they are certain to come. The worst kinds of penalties are those that are stored up over the longest time. Just because you aren't experiencing them now doesn't mean they're not coming.

God knows that the forbidden woman can seem delightfully tempting, and he warns us how dangerously threatening she really is. But the passage does not stop there. Once again, God keeps our minds moving forward—to the possibility of another way of life, an alternative to the pleasures of porn:

> Drink water from your own cistern,
>> running water from your own well.
> Should your springs overflow in the streets,
>> your streams of water in the public squares?
> Let them be yours alone,
>> never to be shared with strangers.
> May your fountain be blessed,
>> and may you rejoice in the wife of your youth.
> A loving doe, a graceful deer—
>> may her breasts satisfy you always,
>> may you ever be intoxicated with her love.
> Why, my son, be intoxicated with another man's
>> wife?
>> Why embrace the bosom of a wayward woman?
>
> *Proverbs 5:15–20*

After giving an honest picture of the temptations and dangers of the wayward woman, God doesn't spend time focusing on simply avoiding her evils. As we saw at the beginning of this chapter, focusing on our sin keeps our minds and our desires trapped. Instead, God advances from a consideration of the forbidden woman to a contemplation of the lovely wife.

## From Danger to Delight: The Lovely Wife

As God turns the page from the forbidden woman of pornography to the lovely wife of biblical marriage, he makes several observations about this new woman.

First, God makes clear that the intimate relationship of marriage is to be shared with no one else. He compares the marriage relationship to a fountain and states, "Should your springs overflow in the streets, your streams of water in the public squares? Let them be yours alone, never to be shared with strangers." The spring of sexuality is to be shared between you and your wife. You are not supposed to partake of water from anyone else's well or let them share yours. The call to be married is the call to fight for an exclusive sexual relationship shared with nobody else.

Next, God tells us we are to rejoice in the wife of our youth. I have no statistics on how long the average career is for actresses in pornography, but I'll bet it's pretty short. I'm confident there are no porn actresses who are sixty years old. Probably not even forty. Why not? Because selfish men who consume porn like their women young. For such men, there's no interest in wrinkles, liver spots, or white hair. There's no attraction in crow's-feet, varicose veins, and sagging skin. In other words, there's no interest in *real* women—women who grow older and suffer health problems. As soon as time steals away the youthful faces and tight bodies of a porn actress, the men who used to ogle them find them gross and disgusting.

This is a sinister corruption of God's plan for how men are to treat women. A man is created for a lifelong covenantal relationship with a woman. They marry, raise children together, and enjoy life together in a relationship of mutual trust, respect, and faith in God. A man's life is not designed to be an endless search for different women, always on the prowl for those who are younger and more attractive. In 1989, Steven Curtis Chapman recorded a song titled "I Will

Be Here" about staying devoted to his wife until they were parted by death. As Chapman reflected about growing old with his wife, he sang, "I will be here to watch you grow in beauty." Men who are obsessed with porn cannot understand what this means. Their conception of beauty is dependent on the appearance of a woman on a screen or in a magazine. It cares nothing for the beauty of character, of dependence in relationship, of faithfulness and shared intimacy over many years together. A man is created to marry a woman and to *grow* in love for the wife of his youth as they each grow older together. God commands this because he wants you to love your wife's whole person, not just her outward appearance. God commands this because he has designed this kind of love to be the most deeply satisfying kind of love, far sweeter than the honeyed lips of the adulterous woman.

Finally, God states that you are to be satisfied with the physical body of your wife. The language in this passage is some of the most sexually explicit in all of Scripture. God commands you to be satisfied in the breasts of your wife. God commands that you delight in the sexual parts of your spouse. The passage goes even further, however, when it declares, "May you ever be intoxicated with her love." Though drunkenness is a sin in the Bible, God commands it here! Not to be drunk with alcohol, but to be drunk with her love. God fully endorses sexual delight in marriage. God does not hate sex; he hates *faithless* sex with forbidden women, but he loves faithful sexual expressions in the context of marriage. God loves it so much that he commands, not just that it happen, but that it be enjoyed to the point of intoxication. Even if your marriage is distant or your passion for each other weak, you should hear this command as good news. God will not command something without supplying the grace and strength to obey it. There is grace for you to delight in your spouse the way God desires.

## Using This Truth as a Grace-Filled Strategy for Change

In Proverbs 5, God does more than show us the ugliness of the forbidden woman and the beauty of the lovely wife. God gives us a strategy for change. In this passage, God acknowledges the temptation and the danger of the forbidden woman, but he doesn't stop there. He ushers our thinking forward to a consideration of holy sexual delight within marriage. He moves from the forbidden woman to the lovely wife.

In other words, God wants you to quit thinking about porn and start thinking about your wife.

You need to learn to stop focusing on porn (even when you're thinking about how much you hate it) and start focusing on your wife. Whenever your thoughts begin to drift toward porn, see this mental drift as an alarm reminding you to pray for grace to refocus your thoughts on your spouse. Proverbs 5 gives three suggestions as you seek grace to do this.

1. *Rejoice in the wife of your youth.* What do you love about your wife? What about her thrills you to rejoicing? Even if you have a difficult or distant marriage, you should be able to think of some things that make you happy about your wife. Maybe you love her giggle, or the food she cooks, or how great a mother she is. Perhaps you delight in her sense of humor, her walk with Christ, or the way she serves others. Think of at least five things, and when you're tempted

to think about porn, pray through the list and ask God to fill you with joyful love for your wife.

2. *Pour energy into your relationship with your wife.* Earlier we saw that God commands us not to give our energies to the forbidden woman. Instead we should use our strength to love and serve our wives. What does your wife appreciate? Perhaps she likes it when you make the bed in the morning, get breakfast for the kids, or do the dishes. Maybe she likes flowers, caresses, dinners out, or short retreats when you can be alone together. Pay attention to your wife and make a list of three small things you can do to serve her every day. When you're tempted to serve yourself by dwelling on porn, pray for grace to serve your wife by doing some of the things on your list.

3. *Direct your sexual energies toward your wife.* It's important that this one come after the two I've just mentioned. If you're not nurturing a heart full of love for your wife on the inside and serving her consistently on the outside, directing your sexual desires toward her will just perpetuate the sexual selfishness of indulging in porn. The fruit of sexual expression is only fully enjoyed by the one who cares well for the roots and shoots of the entire plant. You can't enjoy the blossom of sex without caring for the larger plant in your relationship with your wife. Once you do this, however, sex should be a regular and thrilling part of your marriage. Whenever you find your thoughts flirting with the form of a forbidden woman, pray for grace to desire the physical body of your wife. Think about her and how she looks. Think about what she does that makes you happy. Then pursue her in a winsome and servant-hearted way. Be willing to consider conversations with her about how to have sex become a more regular part of your relationship if it's not.

## What If You Are Single?

Many of you are single and have legitimate questions about how the teachings in this chapter can be of any use for you. I want to share two ways that a consideration of marriage can be helpful for singles battling porn.

First, Proverbs 5 commends marriage, not only to married couples, but also to single individuals. Marriage is wonderful for many reasons, not least because it is the only acceptable environment for sexual intimacy. For this reason, the apostle Paul tells single people that if they cannot control themselves, they should marry, "for it is better to marry than to burn with passion" (1 Corinthians 7:9). Paul does not mean that marriage is the cure for lust. It isn't. He means that marriage is the only legitimate relationship for those with appropriate sexual desires. If you are experiencing God-given sexual desires, a consideration of Proverbs 5 should encourage you to pursue marriage to a godly woman in a wise and careful way. Consider whether being married is truly a priority in your life. Are you putting career goals or other pursuits ahead of a God-given calling to pursue a wife and raise a family? It may be time to reorient your priorities and pursue marriage.

Second, some of you may never marry or you may be so far from it right now that it is not a helpful strategy to encourage you toward it. If that's where you're at, then the Bible has even better news for you! In Ephesians 5, Paul explains the nature and purpose of marriage. Toward the end of his teaching he boils down everything he's written with a summary statement: "I am talking about Christ and the church" (Ephesians 5:32). In other words, everything the Bible says about marriage is not ultimately about marriage at all. God made marriage to point people to the gospel of Jesus Christ. Husbands and wives exist to reflect the saving purposes of Christ for his bride, the church. Marriage is an arrow that points to the reality of Christ's love for the church. Marriage is a shadow whose substance is the saving purpose of Jesus.

This means that though you have legitimate, God-given sexual desires, you do not *need* marriage in any essential way. Marriage is wonderful, and it's important. But the primary reason God created marriage is to picture for us the gospel of Jesus. If you see and grasp the target, you don't need the arrow. If you have the substance, you don't need the shadow.

God created marriage to give the world a glimpse of the gospel of Jesus Christ. Husbands are supposed to love and be devoted to their wives so that people can see the love of Jesus. If you don't have a wife, you are freed up to pour your attention and energy exclusively into Christ and his church in much the way a married man should attend to his wife. You're empowered to be devoted to the substance without being distracted by the shadow. You can devote all of your strength to the expansion of Christ's kingdom as you await his marriage supper (Revelation 19:6–9).

## Accountability in Marriage?

One final note on fighting for purity in your marriage: You may have noticed that this chapter didn't address the topic of having your wife be an accountability partner. That's intentional. I don't think your wife should fill that role. You should treat your wife as your wife. She should be free to treat you as her husband. It is a deadly poison for a marriage when a wife becomes a cop policing her husband's activity, asking him all kinds of questions, and examining his Internet reports. Your wife needs to know you have a faithful accountability partner doing those things so she can have peace of mind as she focuses her energy on being married to you. That's why the focus of this chapter is on laying hold of purity by pursuing your wife as your best friend and lover.

Whether you're married or not, *the key principle has to do with directing your mental and physical energies away from porn and toward the purity of marriage and the Savior to whom marriage points.* This is hard work. It's more difficult than just putting a filter on your computer. The reason it's so hard is that nobody can ever be certain if you're doing it or not. But remember that Jesus knows. He sees the heart, the motives, the truth behind your actions. And he calls you to trust him and to lay hold of his forgiving and transforming grace that alone can equip you to achieve victory in this area.

# Fighting for Purity with the Power of Grace

1.  How have you been guilty of being drawn to the temptations of the forbidden woman in Proverbs 5? In what ways have you refused to believe what the Bible says about how dangerous she is? Confess these sins to the Lord and be drawn to believe in his forgiving grace.

2.  If you're married, consider where you need God's transforming grace to desire your wife. If you're single, consider where you need that same grace to serve Christ wholeheartedly and to reflect on the gospel that saves you. Pray and ask God to give you his powerful transforming grace to empower you to be different in this way.

3.  Share each of these prayers in your accountability relationships. Seek their encouragement, wisdom, and prayers for you in this area.

4.  Turn your thoughts to God's Word. If you're married, spend some time reading through Proverbs 31:10 – 31, and ask God for the grace to help you desire the godly wife it discusses. If you're single, do the same with 1 Corinthians 7:32 – 35.

# CHAPTER 7

# Using Humility to Fight Pornography

Thus far, whenever I have shared a story, I have not used real names. But in this chapter I want to begin with a story about a man whose identity I will *not* conceal. He is called Diotrephes, and he lived in the first century. I know, a moniker like that makes you wonder what his parents had against names like Hank or Larry. Still, as bad as his name was, that is not even the worst thing about this guy.

Diotrephes was a very wicked man.

Diotrephes was a professing Christian in the earliest days of the Christian church, but he did not appreciate the teaching of the apostles. He spread malicious gossip about their ministry. He refused to welcome new Christians when they came to church. And if other Christians tried to welcome these new believers, Diotrephes would seek to expel them from the church.

We learn about Diotrephes when we read the apostle John's third letter (3 John). In summarizing the evil deeds of Diotrephes, John simply says that he "loves to be first" (3 John 9). This is an amazingly sober assessment of such a man. Diotrephes hated the apostles. He refused to welcome new Christians. He punished those who didn't follow his advice because he was infatuated with himself and wanted to be first. He was obsessed with control, with power, with wanting attention for himself. Self-obsession can drive a multitude of sins.

Why do I mention Diotrephes? As a pastor, professor, and counselor, I talk with countless men who struggle with sexual immorality. Though many of these struggles are similar, the details in each case are unique. They have different family histories, different strengths and weakness, and even different reasons for looking at pornography. But even with all these differences, they all share one commonality: like Diotrephes, *they love to be first.*

## Only Arrogant Men Look at Pornography

Here is the point I want you to get in this chapter: *If you look at pornography, you are arrogant.* Does that sound harsh to you? At first, you might think I'm crazy to make a statement like that. After all, when you look at porn, you feel terrible, sad, and trapped. Your actions may not feel all that prideful or arrogant, but I want to help you understand that at the root of what you do is a seed of arrogance. Consider James 3:13–16:

> Who is wise and understanding among you? Let them show it by their good life, by deeds done in the humility that comes from wisdom. But if you harbor bitter envy and selfish ambition in your hearts, do not boast about it or deny the truth. Such "wisdom" does not come down from heaven but is earthly, unspiritual,

demonic. For where you have envy and selfish ambition, there you find disorder and every evil practice.

In this passage, James is encouraging his readers to show
wisdom in the form of good conduct and humility. He commands them to avoid boasting about envy and selfish ambition. James wants Christians to avoid these things because
they are at odds with the humility he is commending. He
says that disorder and vile practices are rooted in envy and
selfishness. In other words, every bad thing you do flows
from an arrogant heart that is selfishly ambitious. If looking
at pornography is an evil practice (and it is!), then it must
flow from a heart that is full of envy, selfish ambition, and
arrogance. The choice is simple and clear: you can look at
porn, or you can be humble. But you cannot do both.

I have found that understanding this connection can be
truly revolutionary in the fight for freedom. Many people
try to help people with porn problems by turning them into
victims. Perhaps you see yourself that way—as a victim of
your upbringing or your circumstances, trapped in a cycle
from which you are powerless to escape. Some may want to
convince you that porn isn't really about sex but about the
brokenness that flows from being lonely. They want you to
think that deep in your soul there is a kind of tank that's
supposed to be full of love—but yours is empty. They argue
that in your neediness you try to fill up that tank with porn.
While I appreciate brothers and sisters in the Lord who sincerely want to help, such teaching simply isn't true. There
are some men who struggle with pornography because they
are lonely and some who do feel unloved, but there is nothing about loneliness and lovelessness that *necessarily* leads
to looking at immoral images. There are plenty of men who

look at porn who are not lonely, and plenty of lonely men who don't look at porn.

Men look at pornography out of an arrogant desire to see women in a way that God does not allow. They show arrogant defiance to God's commands, rejecting the delight of sexual intimacy in marriage and deciding for themselves what they believe is better—looking at naked women in porn. They show arrogant disregard for God's call to selfless marital love. They show arrogant derision for the female actresses whom they should be seeking to respect as women who need to hear the good news of Jesus. They show arrogant disdain for their own children by hiding their sin and inviting the enemy into their home and their marriage. They show arrogant disrespect toward all those who would be scandalized if their sin were known. The root problem with men who look at porn is not neediness—it is arrogance.

I realize this is not a popular message. And I am not trying to hit you over the head with this. I long for those who are enslaved to their sinful lust to be set free. But our culture misunderstands the real problem behind porn addiction and offers the wrong solution. The whole point of this book is to show you that God provides you with his powerful forgiving and transforming grace. His transforming grace is available, but first we need to understand the *actual* problem we have. If you misunderstand your problem and think it is simply a matter of filling your emptiness or addressing your neediness, you will never experience the fullness of God's power to change you. It's only when you rightly understand that selfish ambition is at the root of your sexual sin that the full power of grace will be set loose in your life to change you. This passage in James is actually good news for struggling porn addicts! It correctly identifies the deep corruption in your heart and illuminates where you need to expend energy fighting for God's grace to change.

# From Hubris to Humility

It is impossible to look at porn and be humble. Because this is true, it gives us a key weapon in the fight against porn. As you fight to cultivate a heart of humility, you will also be severing the root of arrogance and selfish ambition that allows pornography to flourish in your life. If you are to be finally free from pornography, you must know how to pursue a humble heart. A heart full of humility takes a lifetime to nurture, so you will not fully achieve it until you are with Christ. But as you fight this battle, there are three areas to consider that will get you started.

## Consider SALVATION

There is nothing that fosters humility like a consideration of what God has done for us in saving us from the consequences of our sin. The entire Bible shows us this truth, but let's look at just one passage right now:

> At one time we too were foolish, disobedient, deceived and enslaved by all kinds of passions and pleasures. We lived in malice and envy, being hated and hating one another. But when the kindness and love of God our Savior appeared, he saved us, not because of righteous things we had done, but because of his mercy. He saved us through the washing of rebirth and renewal by the Holy Spirit, whom he poured out on us generously through Jesus Christ our Savior, so

that, having been justified by his grace, we might
become heirs having the hope of eternal life.

*Titus 3:3–7*

This passage reminds us of the *mercy* of God. It begins by looking at who we are before we become Christians. When Paul says we were foolish and disobedient, he is saying we were displeasing to God in our internal thinking and in our external behavior. Being deceived and enslaved to passions and pleasures means we were led astray from God and shackled to all kinds of created things, serving their interests instead of serving God. Paul also says that before we know Christ, we live in malice and envy. Malice means I want bad things for you, and envy means I want your good things for myself. Finally, Paul describes the pre-conversion state by saying we are hated by others and we hate others. In other words, before we belong to Christ, we are an ugly mess.

But Paul doesn't stop there. In addition to reminding us who are before knowing Christ, Paul reminds of what God has done in saving us. God's kindness, love, and mercy appeared in Christ to save us—apart from any good things we have done. Paul makes it crystal clear that we aren't saved because of any good deeds we have done, *because we don't do good deeds*. We were foolish, disobedient, and enslaved to our sin. There was nothing good we could hope to do! This means our salvation is not something we deserve from God. It's not something he is obligated to do for us, nor is it something we merit.

When you truly grasp the depth of your sin and how undeserving you are of the mercy of God, you should begin to wonder why God would ever bother to save terrible, evil, rebellious people like you and me. The answer is because he is good. He is kind. He is merciful. He saves us to reveal himself to us as a God of mercy. He knows that the only way a holy God and a rebellious person can be reconciled is by restoring the right kind of relationship, one in which we live in humble dependence on our Creator. That begins with our salvation. God shows us we are saved apart from works. Our salvation is entirely dependent on him.

The salvation we have received is described in further detail when Paul says that our redemption includes the washing and renewal of the Holy Spirit. God gave the Spirit to effect his forgiving ("washing") and transforming ("renewal") grace.

Child of God, consider your salvation and be humbled! You were a foul and wretched sinner. Your life was defined by rebellion and hatred. You were lost, lacking any ability to gain salvation for yourself. In your pitiful state, the love, goodness, and kindness of God appeared in the person of Jesus Christ to save you. This salvation happened, not because of any good thing you have done, but simply because God is loving, kind, and merciful. He didn't have to save you. You did nothing to deserve it. And it would have been perfectly just for God to leave you in your sin, condemned for all of eternity.

But he didn't.

That's the good news that sets sinners free. It should humble you to realize that someone as wicked and rebellious as you is the recipient of such amazing love and undeserved mercy.

## Consider SIN

Paul also shows us in the passage from his letter to Titus that it is impossible to consider your salvation without considering your sin. Taking a good, hard look at our sin makes it possible to fully grasp the depth of our salvation, and this has benefits in our pursuit of humility.

I had been counseling Tim for several months about his battle against pornography. Things were going well for him. Since we had begun our times together he had gone from looking at pornography all the time to never looking at it. He had reconciled with his wife, Beth, and the two of them were now fully restored in that area of their marriage. Tim was learning to battle lustful thoughts when they entered his mind and was combating moments of temptation when they first showed up.

Still, I was concerned.

There was evidence of God's transforming grace in Tim's life, but something else was wrong. For starters, he had adopted a critical spirit with Beth. During our times together, I had observed him nitpicking her, and I knew from their conversations that his critical spirit was even worse when I wasn't around. It was nearly impossible to have Tim acknowledge any wrongdoing in his marriage, yet he was quite zealous to label Beth's mistakes as sins. In addition, he had adopted a heavy hand toward his children, and he was increasingly becoming critical with other people, some of whom who had been his friends for years. Tim was an arrogant man.

Tim was like a number of other men I have counseled, and at the very beginning of my ministry I was perplexed by the pattern. I regularly found that men who were legitimately advancing in their fight to be free from pornography were demonstrating profound levels of arrogance in other areas of their life. I've now seen this problem surface often enough that I expect it to happen with the men I counsel as they begin their fight against porn. There are different reasons for this, many of which are peculiar to individual men. But I have found one common trait shared by these men as they struggle with arrogance: *men who struggle with pornography often see pornography as their only sin.*

Men who struggle with pornography are overwhelmed by the degree to which this struggle dominates every area of their life. They feel like they are struggling with it *all* the time—when they are home by themselves, alone in their office, or out of town. Like an unshakable shadow, the struggle seems ever present. And for many of these men, when they think about being a sinner, they immediately think about their struggle with pornography. Pornography is so all-consuming that it drives away any consideration of other sins. This was certainly the case with Tim. When asked to consider sin in his life, all he thought about was his desire to see porn. When the only sin a man sees in his life is his pornography, something fascinatingly sinister happens as he begins to gain victory over that sin: *he believes his sin has gone away.* No more porn comes to mean no more sin. I have never actually heard a man make this statement, but I have seen many who live it out.

If you want to cut the root of porn with the ax of humility, you must consider the other sins in your life as well. You are sinful in more ways than one. You have other problems besides the desire to see pornographic images. It will be good for your soul and for your growth in Christ to consider other sins besides the one that has you reading this book. It is humbling to consider other sins for which you need the forgiving and transforming grace of Jesus. Are you untrustworthy in your friendships? Have you been dishonest in your financial dealings? Do you gossip about the decisions of your church leaders? Are you harsh with your wife or girlfriend? Are you lazy in prayer and Bible study? Are you given to gluttony? Do you have a sluggish work ethic? All these and more are areas where Christ wants to change you. Pursue the humility that comes with considering these neglected areas of your life, and then trust in God's power to change you.

## Consider SERVICE

If you look at porn, you are arrogant. The arrogance of viewing porn is obvious when you consider how selfishly you're using your time. Every second you spend looking at porn is a second you cannot spend serving others. While you're gorging yourself on images of naked women, you're not buying flowers for your wife, cutting the grass of a sick neighbor, buying a meal for an elderly couple, helping your parents with work around the house, inviting a coworker to dinner to share the gospel with him, teaching your child about the Bible, cleaning the dishes after dinner, playing hide-and-seek with your kids, or visiting a church member in the hospital. To such selfish people, God urges, "Do nothing out of selfish ambition or vain conceit. Rather, in humility value others above yourselves, not looking to your own interests but each of you to the interests of the others" (Philippians 2:3–4).

Paul is concerned about ambitions motivated by selfish desires. He is concerned that we not become driven by vain conceit. He is concerned that we do nothing out of arrogance or pride. Paul commends Christians to combat these self-consuming attitudes with humility—valuing others above oneself. Paul indicates that the way to do this is by radically shifting your focus away from your own interests to the interests of others.

Stop and think about this for a moment. Have you ever considered how extraordinarily practical this counsel is? Paul doesn't just say, "Be humble!" He tells us how to cultivate humility—by learning to prioritize other people's interests above our own.

When your alarm goes off in the morning, you probably start cycling through all the things you have to do that day: take a shower, have your devotional time, get to work, get to school, meet with the boss, get the car serviced, catch up with a friend, finish a project, get home and eat dinner, mow the lawn, and do some work on your computer. Our lives are filled with important things we *need* to be doing, and our to-do lists fill up our available time. We grow irritated when a friend calls with a question that takes time to answer, or when an aged parent asks us for help with something at the house, or when a child's question interrupts our concentration. We are entirely focused on pursuing our own interests.

In the midst of such a welter of activity Paul gives this very practical exhortation: look not only to your own interests but look beyond your own interests to the interests of others. Don't cycle through your to-do list like it's the only thing that matters. God also wants you to consider the interests of other people. What on your wife's plate can you help with? Are your parents struggling in an area where you can assist? Is a coworker under the gun and in need of your cooperation, even though it's not in your job description? Could a friend borrow your car while theirs is in the shop, even though you had places you wanted to go?

Serving others is part of the daily life of every Christian, but it is particularly urgent for men who habitually look at pornography. Looking at porn doesn't affect just your own life. It's not a victimless crime, because instead of serving others you are inflicting harm on them. Rather than serving your spouse (or future spouse), you are damaging the purity and sanctity of that relationship. Instead of loving those who love you, you are storing up pain for the time when they discover all you've been doing in secret. The antidote to this selfishness involves more than just avoiding pornography. True repentance means replacing pornography with something else, something that honors God and demonstrates love to others. You must begin humbly looking to the interests of others and seeking ways to serve them.

## Humility Requires Grace

We will not be completely humble until we see Jesus face-to-face. Being humble isn't easy. Like Diotrephes, we want to be first. This desire to be first is the root of indwelling sin. As James reminds us, every vile practice comes out of a heart that is selfishly ambitious. This means that all of our battles against sin are essentially battles against our arrogant hearts. This principle is as true for pornography as for any other sin. Where can we find the power and motivation to wage war against a foe embedded so deeply in our hearts?

The promise we repeatedly return to is the gospel—that God gives us his grace to forgive and change us into new people. God gives us his power to be cleansed from our arrogant conceit when we name our sin, ask him to forgive our sin, and believe we are forgiven and cleansed from it. God gives us his power to obey when we believe that the blood of Jesus empowers our efforts at humility. By believing, we receive God's own power to be forgiven of the spirit of Diotrephes, who loved to be first, and the power to possess the spirit of Christ, who promises that the first will be last, and the last first.

# Fighting for Purity with the Power of Grace

1. Do you recognize areas of arrogance in your life that lead to pornography, and are you convicted by this arrogance? Ask the Lord's forgiveness, and seek his power to grow in humility.

2. Spend time praying through Titus 3:1 – 7 and ask the Lord to open your eyes to the saving work he has accomplished in your life. Pray for a humble spirit as you consider your sin and his mercy to you.

3. Make a list of other sins you need to work on in your life besides pornography. Talk with your accountability partner, spouse, parents, or others and ask them to help you identify patterns of sinfulness in your life that exist outside the area of sexual purity. Take time to pursue God's grace to forgive and change in this area. Work with your accountability partner to develop a plan to begin growing in those areas.

4. Consider some ways you can begin to serve others in your sphere of influence, and then make a list of four specific ways you can serve. In addition to planning opportunities to serve, use your list when you are tempted so you have something profitable to do rather than indulging your selfish desire to see pornography. Seek God's grace to forgive and empower when you don't desire to serve.

# CHAPTER 8

# Using Gratitude to Fight Pornography

Dustin had changed. Since he and I first began meeting together, the Lord had begun to set him free from the addiction to pornography that had completely dominated his life. Back then, Dustin was so trapped in his sin that he couldn't imagine going a single day without looking at pornography for at least several hours. This life-dominating sin led to all kinds of difficulties in his life. He almost lost his job because of frequent absences from work. He would have likely been fired if his boss had known Dustin was not really sick as he had claimed, but was spending his time looking at porn. Dustin was experiencing difficulties with his wife, who knew about his problem, was committed to him, and wanted help, but was full of despair and convinced that things would never change. On top of all this, Dustin was constantly depressed, feeling distant from his wife, his friends, and, most importantly, the Lord. When he wasn't depressed, he felt numb. Life seemed to have lost any sense of vibrant joy or purpose.

But things had changed. Dustin hadn't looked at pornography for almost a year. He was in a growing relationship with the Lord and enjoying a closer walk with Christ than he had ever known in his life as a Christ follower. He was restored to his wife, and they were experiencing more joy in their marriage than ever before. The fight for purity hadn't been easy. There had certainly been struggles and battles to fight along the way, but there was no denying that the change God had worked was profound.

Dustin and I talked one afternoon about how kind the Lord had been to change him. I asked him to share what he considered the most significant milestones on his journey to freedom. He mentioned two things. The most important factor, he said, was learning how to draw near to Jesus, which is what we'll look at in the next chapter. This wasn't much of a surprise to him, as he knew he had grown distant from Christ and needed to draw near to him again. But the second milestone he shared was something he hadn't anticipated at all. Dustin was surprised to discover that one of the most significant areas of growth for him on the road to freedom was learning to be *thankful*.

## The Importance of Gratitude in the Fight for Freedom

In Paul's letter to the Ephesians, God shows us how powerful a spirit of gratitude can be as a weapon in the fight against pornography:

> But among you there must not be even a hint of sexual immorality, or of any kind of impurity, or of greed, because these are improper for God's holy people. Nor

should there be obscenity, foolish talk or coarse joking, which are out of place, *but rather thanksgiving.*

*Ephesians 5:3–4, emphasis added*

In this passage we see that God forbids all kinds of impurity, actions, and thoughts that do not reflect being holy and
set apart as God's people. Earlier, we saw that God forbids
impure speech — ruling out obscenity, foolish talk, and
coarse joking. God wants his people to be pure in what they
say. Therefore, whenever we speak about sex or our sexual
struggles, we must seek to do so in a way that is respectful
of others and honoring to God.

But impure speech isn't the only kind of immorality God
forbids. He also forbids all kinds of sexual immorality. In
addition to pure speech, three specific areas are emphasized.

*First, God forbids actions that are obviously sexually immoral.*
In fact, he says that those who are pursuing purity should
not have "even a hint" of this kind of sexual immorality in
their lives. Adultery, fornication, and viewing pornography
are examples of what is forbidden here.

*Second, God forbids any kind of impurity.* God strengthens
his previous command to avoid sexual immorality. This command is especially relevant for those who want to push out
the boundary lines of purity as far as they can. Today, some
argue that unless you had sexual intercourse you haven't had
sex. In fact, I've talked to many young men and women who
answer questions about their purity with statements like,
"Well, we didn't have *sex*, but . . ." Instead of trying to get as
close to the line as we can without crossing over, we should
cultivate a love for purity in *every* area of life, not just sexual
purity. To those who want to push the line, getting as close
to sin as they can, God urges that they turn around and head
in the opposite direction — to get as far away as possible!

*Third, God forbids greed.* God strengthens his command against sexual immorality by forbidding any kind of impurity, and he strengthens both of these commands by forbidding greed. The use of the word *greed* in this context might be confusing if you always equate greed with money. But greed covers more than just a powerful desire for money. Greed has to do with covetousness, sinful desire, and evil lusts. You can be greedy for all kinds of things — money, food, power, or, as Paul includes in the context here, sex. Talking about greed strengthens the other commands forbidding sexual immorality and impurity because by forbidding greed, God is directly addressing the kind of heart that drives all of these immoral and impure behaviors. Not only should we avoid sexually immoral behavior; we should avoid having a heart that is greedy for them. Jesus makes the same point when he teaches that the sin of adultery begins with the lust that fuels it in the heart (Matthew 5:27–28).

In Ephesians 5, we see that God forbids all kinds of sexual immorality. He forbids sexually immoral speech, sexually immoral acts, the impure behaviors that push the lines toward those acts, and the greedy hearts that desire those acts. But God does not just *forbid* in this passage; he also *commends*. God says that in place of immorality there should be something else, and that something else is thankfulness.

Don't skip past this. Settle in on this idea, and let it sink down deep for a few minutes. It may be the key strategy God wants to use to set you free from your addiction to pornography. In this passage, God is urging Christians to replace sexual immorality with something else. He could have inspired the apostle Paul to write any number of things here: "but rather *love*" or *mercy* or *self-control* or *joy*. Instead of any of those wonderful things, God wanted Paul to tell Christians to replace immorality with *thanksgiving*. This means we need to consider why gratitude is so important to God in the fight against sexually immoral acts like pornography.

## The Opposite of Gratitude is Greed

Paul wants Christians to fight for thanksgiving in their struggle for purity because a greedy heart is at the root of sexual immorality and impurity. The only time people are immoral and impure is when they are greedy for things that are immoral and impure. Take away the greedy heart that desires immorality, and those evil actions will also go away. Paul sees something unique about gratitude that has the power to destroy the greedy lust gripping the heart. We can better understand the connection between greed and gratitude when we grasp their opposite natures.

Greedy lust wants what it does not have. Of course, it's not necessarily wrong to want things you don't have. If you're hungry, it's good to want a sandwich. If you're thirsty, it's right to desire some water. When you're tired, there's nothing wrong with longing for a good night's sleep. Greedy lust, however, perverts desire either in *degree* or in *direction*. Greed perverts desire in degree when you want a good thing too much. If you're hungry and want a sandwich so badly that you're short-tempered with the server at the deli, or if you're thirsty and want a drink so badly that you don't share with others who are thirsty, then your good desire is perverted in degree. Greed perverts desire in direction when you want things you shouldn't want or you want to satisfy your desire in the wrong way. Sexual desire is not sinful in itself, but when you desire sex with a woman who is not your spouse, your desire is pointed in the wrong direction and is lustful.

In contrast, gratitude is the attitude of a heart that is thankful for anything and everything the Lord gives. You are grateful when you are glad for and content with what you have. Thankfulness is the opposite of lust because the thankful heart has stopped prowling around for everything it doesn't have and is overwhelmed with appreciation for all the good things it already possesses. The logic of lust requires you to be discontent with what you have and pay attention to all the things you don't have. The logic of thankfulness requires you to focus on what you have already received and to be overcome with thanks. Gratitude is the opposite of greed.

This is more than a true principle or an interesting contrast; it is also a strategy for defeating sin. God doesn't only make known to us the truth that greed and gratitude are opposites. He commands us to *stop being greedy* and *start being grateful*. In a war it's not enough to defend against the attack of an aggressor. Ultimately, we must take offensive measures to be victorious. Gratitude is the offensive weapon that destroys the enemy stronghold of greed that is at the source of your desire for pornography. When you begin to destroy greed with gratitude, you're not far from freedom.

## Learning to Be Thankful

If you struggle with porn, one of your greatest needs is to grow in the grace of gratitude. Just because you may never have thought about this doesn't mean it isn't true. Porn is only consumed by thankless people. The desire for porn is a desire to escape from what the Lord has given you into a fake universe full of things you do not have and will never have. Porn is the trading of gratitude for greed. Porn trades joy in the reality God has graced you with for greed in the counterfeit world he has not. Defeating porn requires a grateful consideration of God's good gifts to you.

You have a wonderful and precious life given to you from the good hand of God himself. He has given things to you that he has given to no other person. They are yours and yours alone for the few precious moments you have in this life. Every second you spend lusting after the women in porn is a priceless treasure given away and is a distraction from glad thankfulness in the life you have. While you long for the women of porn who are not yours, you fail to consider all the things that *are* yours.

The Lord has given you precious friends to love and family relationships to steward. All of us know people who care for us. Whether friends, parents, children, cousins, or spiritual leaders, we are all in relationships. Think of these people for a moment and be grateful for them. Perhaps you have wonderful parents who have cared for you well and served you in every way they can. Maybe you have kids whose joy and energy fill your life with happiness. I'll bet you have a best friend with whom you love to laugh—a friend you enjoy being with in good times and bad. These relationships are a gift that you should think about and be thankful for.

Do you have a wife? If so, the Lord has given her to you to love and cherish. Think of your wife for a moment and be grateful. Consider her laugh and her smile; ponder her physical body, which God designed especially for you as a gift to be enjoyed; think about the friends she has and all the things they admire about her; remember your wedding night; contemplate the tender moments you've shared with no other person but her. Even if your marriage has difficulties, God has given you your wife as a gift. Reflect on this gift and be thankful.

What ministry has the Lord given you? The Lord calls all of his people to use their gifts and talents in his service—regardless of whether your ministry is a paid position. What gifts has he given you to steward? What responsibilities has he placed on your shoulders? Think of this for a moment and be grateful. When was the last time you thanked God for the opportunities to use the gifts he has given to you? When was the last time you thanked him for the people in your sphere of influence who appreciate the way you minister to them? When was the last time you thanked God for those in your ministry who have challenged and corrected you? Reflect on these things and be thankful.

All who trust in Christ have a saving relationship with the Lord. When was the last time you considered the great love of the Father in creating you and redeeming you? Your life is an incalculable gift from heaven given to you by God himself. Your salvation was purchased for you by the infinitely valuable blood of Christ. As those who have been made and saved by God, we have received forgiveness for our sins, and infinitely more! We receive Christ's own power to change and become like him. As those who are growing to look like Christ, we get the amazing privilege of being called his servants, his friends, and even his children. Have you considered lately that the saving love of God led to the death of Christ so you could be forgiven and—in a breathtaking display of love—called sons of God?

Every greedy glance at pornography is a missed opportunity to be thankful to the Lord and to others for all the good things in your life.

## The Result of Gratitude Is Gladness

Before Dustin finally changed at a deep level he made many attempts to quit looking at porn—all of which ended in frustration and failure. He tried making promises to himself; he tried accountability; he tried bargaining with God. But none of these attempts worked. Every time Dustin would try one of them, sooner or later he would begin to long for pornography again. He knew it was wrong to want porn, but that didn't seem to matter. His desire to see pornography was so intense that he would stop caring what his wife, friends, or even God thought. Eventually his greedy cravings produced a zealous return to pornography, which in turn would produce the unbearable guilt that followed his indulgence in sin.

There are a number of problems with Dustin's attempts at change. For starters, he was missing the power available to those who trust in God's forgiving and transforming grace. In addition, his life was lacking gladness and joy. Dustin's struggle was a graceless and joyless battle against porn, largely dependent on his own strength. When he wasn't looking at porn he was unhappy because he wanted to be looking at it, and after he indulged he was unhappy because he had looked at it. The thrill of seeing naked women seemed worth it in the moment, but afterward there was no real happiness as he struggled with his accusing conscience and a constant fear of being caught.

People hooked on porn fail to change, even when they

want to, because they believe nothing besides porn will ever make them happy. Like Dustin, they might know their problem is wrong and believe that God somehow has something better for them. Yet, in the moment, they still choose to view porn out of a belief that the joy of looking is better than the joy of not looking. The battle to be free from porn is the battle to find a deeper joy. There are many strategies to pursue this joy. The most significant one is the focus of the next chapter—to learn to delight in God above all else. But as we have seen, the Bible gives us another significant strategy in the fight to be grateful. Greedy lust undercuts gladness, while gratitude produces it.

Lust robs you of gladness. About the time you start to appreciate something you've received, greedy desire begins to look for the next thing. Greedy desire convinces you that you must have that next thing. The promise is that you can't be happy until you have that next thing, and when you finally possess it, you'll finally be happy. It's all a lie. It's the very nature of lust to pursue whatever it doesn't have.

Lust guarantees that as soon as you possess the object of your longing, you will get a new greedy desire for something more. This explains why marriage isn't the cure for lust and masturbation that many singles believe it will be. Once a man has a wife, he starts wanting the next thing that he does not have. This is the vicious cycle of lust. Lust never has what it wants because it never has enough. Lust steals joy by creating an endless state of discontentment in the constant search for that one next thing you don't have yet. Lust is never happy because lust is never full.

This is not the case with gratitude. Gratitude fuels gladness and multiplies it. It is the logic of gratitude to be thankful for what you have instead of longing for what you don't. As you learn to be grateful for whatever God has given (instead of greedily lusting after what he has not), your appreciation will lead to joy.

In Dustin's case, he zealously pursued pornography to fuel his lust. He thought about it and longed for it even when he and his wife had sex together. Dustin eventually came to see that his constant turning to pornography, either in his mind or his behavior, was due to a fundamental lack of gratitude for his wife, Lori. He couldn't have joy in his relationship with his wife because he was never really glad to be with her. He was too busy desiring the images of women he saw in pornography. As Dustin changed, God's grace trained him to grow in gratitude for his wife. He grew in thankfulness for her appearance, her body, and her personality. As he began to appreciate her, he began to desire her rather than desiring everything he *didn't* have. Then, when he was with his wife, he found that his joy had increased because he was now grateful for what he had. His joy in possessing the object of his grateful longing led to yet more gladness and gratitude. Like compounding interest, the benefits kept growing. For Dustin, gratitude led to gladness, and gladness produced gratitude. It will do the same for you.

Perhaps you are longing for the joy that accompanies gratitude and you want to be done with the despair that attends greedy lust. But as you look at your life you don't see much to be grateful for. You may be thinking about all sorts of frustrating realities in your life that make you wonder just what it is that you can be thankful for. Remember 1 Thessalonians 5:18: "Give thanks in all circumstances; for this is God's will for you in Christ Jesus." This verse teaches that because God is always being kind to you, it is always essential to be grateful. It is the will of God for you to be full of gratitude, regardless of your situation.

God will never demand something of you that he will not empower you to do by his grace. You can trust in God's power to bring about change in your life. If you struggle with gratitude, you need to lay hold of God's grace to forgive you of your sinful ingratitude. You also need to trust in his grace to empower you to flee greed and embrace gratitude. And as you trust in the grace of Jesus to do this, you will be closer to freedom than you can imagine.

# Fighting for Purity with the Power of Grace

1. Do you believe your pornographic pursuits are ultimately an expression of greed and a lack of gratitude? If you do, ask God to forgive you for your lusts and to help you grow in the grace of gratitude.

2. Go back and reread the section "Learning to Be Thankful." Make a list of areas in which you can learn to grow in gratitude, including your relationships, the many wonderful opportunities the Lord has given you, and the salvation you have received. Come up with at least ten things for which you can thank God and others. Pray through that list now, and revisit each one when you're tempted to indulge the lustful greed in your heart.

3. Commit to expressing heartfelt thanks to at least three people in the next week. Pray for God's help when this is difficult or undesirable.

4. Share all of this with your accountability partner and seek his input.

# CHAPTER 9

# Using a Dynamic Relationship with Jesus to Fight Pornography

The sun rose over the mountains and ignited the sparkling lake with a fiery orange hue. A massive group of hungry people ambled across the Galilean countryside in search of Jesus. The day before, they had gone out to hear Jesus preach and had grown very hungry as the day went on. Jesus—to their shocked amazement—fed more than five thousand of them with a few loaves and fishes from a little boy's lunch. Shortly thereafter, Jesus departed to the other side of the lake. A day later, as the group moved about the countryside, full bellies had become empty bellies, and the people wanted to find Jesus again. Their search carried them all the way to the other side of the Sea of Galilee, where they finally found Jesus again. John 6 records what happened next.

As the crowd approached Jesus, they asked an innocent-sounding question: "Rabbi, when did you get here?" (verse 25).

Jesus saw right through the small talk and exposed the desire of their hearts.

> Jesus answered, "Very truly I tell you, you are looking for me, not because you saw the signs I performed but because you ate the loaves and had your fill. Do not work for food that spoils, but for food that endures to eternal life, which the Son of Man will give you. For on him God the Father has placed his seal of approval."
>
> *John 6:26–27*

Jesus knew what they were up to. They were interested in bread, not him. Jesus' response was intended to direct their hearts away from food and toward himself.

The people didn't get it. Their ears should have perked up at the promise of eternal life. Their spirits should have soared as they realized they were in the presence of the one who had received the Father's full approval. Missing these staggering realities, the crowd instead focused on their own work, their own efforts. They asked, "What must we do to do the works God requires?" (verse 28). Without directly correcting them, Jesus again redirected their minds from a focus on themselves to a focus on himself. He said, "The work of God is this: to believe in the one he has sent" (verse 29). Jesus' message is obvious—Look to *me*! Believe in *me*!

If you're expecting the people to understand Jesus' point, you're about to be disappointed because they missed it again. You can almost hear their stomachs growling as they respond, "What sign then will you give that we may see it and believe you? What will you do? Our ancestors ate the manna in the wilderness; as it is written: 'He gave them bread from heaven to eat'" (verses 30–31).

Did you catch that?

This crowd just received a summons to trust in the one who has the Father's approval. Hours earlier, they had witnessed him perform the greatest miracle any of them had likely ever seen. Now they want *another* miracle. In fact, their request for another sign is a lame attempt to get more food from Jesus. These people didn't come seeking Jesus; they came seeking a free lunch.

Jesus once again sees their response about miracles and manna as a veiled request for another meal. Jesus describes the fuller meaning behind the manna of Moses' day: "Very truly I tell you, it is not Moses who has given you the bread from heaven, but it is my Father who gives you the true bread from heaven. For the bread of God is the bread that comes down from heaven and gives life to the world" (verses 32–33). The manna they read about in the days of Moses is kids' stuff. God means to give them true bread from heaven that won't just fill the bellies of a crowd for a day, but will give life to the entire world.

True bread from heaven! Bread that would feed not just five thousand men, but the whole world! Bread that doesn't just fill you up for a day, but gives everlasting life! This is some serious bread. Now Jesus has their attention. You can feel the excitement rising as the crowd makes its next request: "'Sir,' they said, 'always give us this bread!'" (verse 34).

We can excuse the crowd for being a bit perplexed when Jesus responds, "I am the bread of life. Whoever comes to me will never go hungry, and whoever believes in me will never be thirsty ... For my Father's will is that everyone who looks to the Son and believes in him shall have eternal life, and I will raise them up at the last day" (verses 35, 40). Jesus wants to make clear that the bread they need is him.

Unfortunately, Jesus is not the bread they were looking for. They wanted bread in their stomachs rather than in their souls. When they complain, asking, "How can this man give us his flesh to eat?" (verse 52), Jesus finally throws the hammer down:

> "Very truly I tell you, unless you eat the flesh of the Son of Man and drink his blood, you have no life in you. Whoever eats my flesh and drinks my blood has eternal life, and I will raise them up at the last day. For my flesh is real food and my blood is real drink. Whoever eats my flesh and drinks my blood remains in me, and I in them. Just as the living Father sent me and I live because of the Father, so the one who feeds on me will live because of me. This is the bread that came down from heaven. Your ancestors ate manna and died, but whoever feeds on this bread will live forever."
>
> *John 6:53–58*

I'll be the first to admit that this passage sounds a bit strange, but if you've been following the conversation thus far, you know that Jesus is not commending cannibalism. Instead, he is speaking in categories that stun his listeners out of their search for food to fill their rumbling bellies. And he is speaking to them in terms that his hungry listeners will understand.

## How Do You Eat and Drink Jesus?

The problem was that Jesus' listeners were obsessed with eating literal bread. Though Jesus tried to point them away from free bread to something far more wonderful, they kept bringing the conversation back to food. So when Jesus tells them to eat his flesh and drink his blood, it's his way of saying to the crowds, "Don't you get it? You are obsessed with bread. You need to be captivated by me. I am what you need. Come to me. Don't look to me for what I can do for you. *Seek me*."

Even when we understand that Jesus' language was meant to shock his audience out of their hunger-driven request for bread, we may still wonder what Jesus means. If Jesus doesn't want us literally to eat and drink his body and blood, how are we to do what he's commanding here? We should notice that just before Jesus tells the people to consume his body and blood, he says something else: "For my Father's will is that everyone who looks to the Son and believes in him shall have eternal life, and I will raise them up at the last day" (John 6:40). In John 6:54, we are told to eat Jesus' flesh and drink his blood to receive eternal life and be raised up; in John 6:40, Jesus says we must look to him and believe in him in order to receive this same life and resurrection.

Putting these two verses together, we see the connection: *we eat and drink Jesus whenever we look to him in faith.* When we believe that Jesus is who he said he is and did what he said he did, we are "consuming" him the way he commands. Jesus commands us to eat and drink him because he is portraying faith in him in graphic terms. Jesus came as a Savior bringing eternal life and salvation to a lost and dying world. He didn't come as a waiter serving bread to a crowd of greedy people.

The reason Jesus performed the miracle of feeding the multitude was not to end their hunger pangs; it was to summon their belief in him as the Son of God who had come in power to deliver people from sin (John 6:26, 29, 32). When we focus on our own interests and desires, we miss the ultimate reason that God provided Jesus to save us. We need to know that the bread we should be consuming is Jesus.

This message runs against the popular grain. It means that Jesus did not come to meet any and every need we might believe we have at any given moment. Some in the church today believe and teach that Jesus' fundamental mission is to meet our perceived needs. So, for example, if you are lonely, Jesus came to be your friend; if you're single, Jesus came to be your companion; if you feel ugly, Jesus came to be your encourager; if you're broke, Jesus came to make you rich; if you're sick, Jesus came to make you well. The crowd in John 6 was hungry and believed Jesus came to make them full.

Now it is gloriously true that Jesus is a friend of sinners. He provides for us, and we can depend on him for our daily bread. Nevertheless, Jesus' entire point in John 6 is to correct those who see him *primarily* as something other than the Savior from sin. Jesus corrects us when we simply want him to make us happy by meeting our "felt" needs. The truth is that we need him as our Savior, the one who can forgive our sins and provide eternal life. Jesus becomes our Savior when we eat his body and drink his blood by looking to him in repentant faith.

## So What Does Any of This Have to Do with Pornography?

You may be wondering how any of this helps you in your struggle against pornography. Why have I spent so much time in the last chapter of this book talking about people seeking bread from Jesus—particularly when you want help combating porn! I believe John 6 has everything to do with pornography. You see, many pursue Jesus in search of help with porn in exactly the same way the crowd pursued Jesus in search of bread.

Many Christians locked in a fight against pornography judge the closeness of their relationship with Christ by whether or not they've looked at porn recently. If you didn't look at porn today, you feel alive and close to Jesus. If you did look at porn today, you feel like garbage and very distant from Christ. When you look at porn, you feel like your prayers (if you pray at all) are all about your porn problem: *Lord, take it away. God, why am I doing this again? I don't want to ruin my life, hurt my family, or lose my ministry. God, please help me get rid of this struggle.* You've probably been deeply frustrated with God, wondering why you're still struggling the way you are. You may have even harbored suspicions about Christ and why he is allowing you to continue to struggle. Perhaps you wonder if Jesus is who he said he is since you still have your problem. You believe that your doubts would lift if he would simply take away your problem on your timetable.

You want Jesus to do a sign for you. Like the crowd that wanted bread, you want Jesus to prove who he is by giving you what you want. Please don't misunderstand—it is good to want Jesus' help in your struggle against porn, and he wants to give you that help. That's what this book is about. It's also good to look to Jesus to give you your daily bread, just as the crowd did in John 6. The people in John 6 were wrong, not because they looked to Jesus for bread, but because *bread is all they wanted from him.* Their error was not in seeking Jesus for bread, but in seeking Jesus for bread *exclusively.* They wanted Jesus to satisfy their physical hunger apart from his larger work of giving them fullness of life in more important areas. They minimized Jesus and his work by seeing him as the source of only one good thing rather than cherishing him as the fountain for all of life.

It is wonderful to seek Jesus for freedom from pornography. Yet in coming to Jesus with this desire, you may be a lot like the crowd looking for mere bread. Your relationship with Christ is defined exclusively by your struggle with porn. This is especially true if you're struggling with disappointment with God because of your porn problem, or if you pray fervently only in the aftermath of looking at pornography. The truth that God wants you to know is that *your relationship with Jesus is bigger than your struggle with porn*. If the only time you're interested in walking with Jesus is when you want his help to get over porn, you're not walking in the fullness of the loving relationship that Jesus wants to have with you.

We all come selfishly to Christ at times. All of us want him to do the things we want on the timetable that seems right to us. We get frustrated when God wisely defies our foolish expectations. It is not Jesus' job to be at our beck and call. This reality doesn't mean you shouldn't look to Jesus to help with your porn problem, to fill your belly with bread, or to supply any other good thing that you truly need. It does mean you shouldn't come seeking the help of an errand boy whose job is to rush in and satisfy your every whim. You should come to the sovereign King of the Universe who graciously saves from sin and gives eternal life and who acts in his own way and in his own timing. You should come pursuing a full-fledged relationship with this sovereign King who saves, desiring to draw close to him in every way, and not just seeking to get your problems fixed. Coming to Christ in this way is tons better than merely getting his help to avoid looking at porn. Coming to Jesus in this way looks to him as the comprehensive Savior that he is rather than just as another Mr. Fix-It.

## From Consumers of Porn to Consumers of Christ

When you grasp the point I'm making, you'll see that the title of this chapter is intentionally ironic. You should not seek a dynamic relationship with Jesus because you want to be finished with porn. You should not seek a dynamic relationship with Jesus for any purpose other than knowing Jesus. Whenever you come to Jesus merely for the stuff he gives you or the tasks he can accomplish for you, you're missing the point of coming to Jesus. Jesus doesn't exist for our sake, though he graciously serves us in our sin. We exist for him, because of him, to worship and serve him.

Though you may initially be drawn to Christ out of your great need to be free from pornography, your struggle against this sin is just the beginning of God's greater purpose in saving you. You are saved, not just to be free from pornography, but to know and experience the joy of walking with Jesus, of following him, and of becoming more and more like him. This is another way of stating what Jesus taught his disciples: "Seek first his kingdom and his righteousness, and all these things will be given to you as well" (Matthew 6:33).

You must learn to focus on seeking God before seeking other things, trusting that when you do, he will give you what you need. It would be wrong to seek the *things* before you seek *him*. Imagine a son who takes advantage of his father. This son is out of work and out of money and only goes to see his dad to ask for financial help. What would you think of such a son? You'd probably say he's a dishonorable young man who doesn't love his father, but only uses him.

Now imagine a son who loves his father. He loves being around his father to share the joys and sorrows of life. He is eager to hear his wisdom and follow his advice. What would you think of this son asking his father for financial help when he fell on hard times? You would likely think it was good that the son had a loving father to help him in times of need, and you would be right. It is a sign of deep, committed love when someone seeks help from someone with whom they have a close relationship. It is a sign of corruption to seek help from someone you only look to when you are in trouble.

You need to be the kind of person who fights for a close relationship with Jesus more than you fight against pornography. Your struggle isn't just to avoid looking at porn. It's much more glorious than that. You have the unspeakable privilege of being invited to have a real relationship with the Savior of your soul who alone has the Father's seal of approval. You get to walk with him. You are honored to pursue him. It is your special benefit to fight to know Christ in personal terms. When you find yourself working to look to Christ more than you find yourself working to avoid porn, you'll know you've turned the corner.

You cannot look at Jesus and look at porn at the same time. You have to stop doing one to do the other. A living, breathing relationship with the Savior of the world will drive porn out of your life quicker than anything else. When you turn your eyes to Jesus, there isn't room for anything else in your heart because he fills it up. When you open the blinds of a pitch-black room, the sunlight drives away the darkness. When you place an unfilled pitcher under a faucet, the water drives away the emptiness. When you visit a lonely friend, your presence drives away the isolation. In the same way, when the presence of Jesus floods your life, he will drive away the impurity of pornography. If you fight to consume Jesus, you will inevitably stop consuming porn, sooner or later.

## Fighting for a Relationship with Jesus

How do we do this? What does it look like to fight for this relationship with Jesus? Jesus gives a hint when he says to the hungry crowd, "Whoever eats my flesh and drinks my blood remains in me, and I in them" (John 6:56). Jesus calls us to remain in him. This idea of remaining in him mirrors the words of Jesus in John 15:7–8: "If you remain in me and my words remain in you, ask whatever you wish, and it will be done for you." For Jesus, remaining in him is identified with two things.

First, we remain in Jesus by having his words remain in us. Since the only place where we receive Jesus' words is in the Bible, we can conclude that we remain in Christ when we pursue hearing him speak in the Scriptures. Every meaningful relationship we have involves hearing from the other person. If we say we have a close association with someone but never listen to that person, then we are not as close as we might think. The same is true of our relationship with Jesus. If we say we love Jesus but never hear from him in the pages of his Word, we need to reconsider whether he is the true friend we assume he is.

Second, we remain in Jesus by asking him whatever we wish. When Jesus talks about asking him for things, he's talking about prayer. Relationships involve both hearing and speaking. In our friendships we hear from and speak to those with whom we are connected. It is the same with Jesus. If you want to fight for a relationship with Jesus, then you should fight to hear from him in the Bible and to speak to him in prayer.

Jesus speaks in the relational category of remaining in him—dwelling with and abiding in him. We often speak of prayer and Bible reading in terms of a list of things to do and a set of disciplines to accomplish. Jesus doesn't do that. When he talks about listening to him and speaking to him, he is inviting us to share in his life. Let me make three suggestions that have helped me in my own effort to remain in Christ.

First, *pray the words of Scripture.* Jesus tells us to ask whatever we wish when his words abide in us. This is an invitation to pray the Bible when we read it. We reap at least two benefits from this approach. On the one hand, it guards against mindlessly skimming the Bible and encourages prayerful consideration of the words of Scripture. The words of the Bible will more readily soak into our hearts when we are turning those words into prayers directed to Christ. On the other hand, it ensures that we are praying prayers that please Christ. You might not know if God wants you to take a particular job or marry a certain person, but you can know from John 15 that he wants you to abide in Christ. When you pray that prayer, you are making a request God loves to grant.

Second, *pray out loud.* I don't know about you, but I can get distracted very easily. My prayers can turn to daydreams quicker than you can say "Amen." One of the most effective ways I have found to stay focused in prayer is to pray out loud. When I speak to anyone else, I speak out loud. Why shouldn't I speak to God that way? When we pray to God like we would speak to another human being—out loud—we may find we can spend more time in focused prayer.

Third, *sing songs to God*. There are plenty of days when I don't feel like praying. I have more stories than I care to share about the coolness of my heart toward encountering Christ in relationship. One thing I find that most typically warms my cold heart is singing songs to God. It's impossible to stay lukewarm when you sing with conviction:

> *Amazing grace! How sweet the sound, that saved a wretch*
> *    like me!*
> *I once was lost, but now am found, was blind, but now I see.*

Your heart will quickly be captivated when you sing with believing passion:

> *My sin—O the bliss of this glorious thought!—*
> *My sin, not in part, but the whole,*
> *Is nailed to the cross and I bear it no more;*
> *Praise the Lord, praise the Lord, O my soul!*

The state of your soul will be changed for good if you can sing joyfully and with faith:

> *Because the sinless Savior died*
> *My sinful soul is counted free.*
> *For God the just is satisfied*
> *To look on him and pardon me.*

Sometimes you're not in a place where you can sing out loud. I have often whispered the lyrics of songs and received the same benefit. God has designed music to lift our souls.

If you're feeling distant from Christ, try singing to him to draw you closer.

Regardless of how you direct your heart toward a relationship with Christ, you must prioritize this task. You must not seek him only for what he can give—even if you are seeking good things. Jesus is not your lapdog. He is your sovereign Savior. Pursue him so you can know him. When the benefit you seek from Jesus is the benefit of knowing him, you can be confident that he will not withhold any other good thing from you—whether in your fight against pornography or in any other circumstance.

In the end, you can't get to Jesus without the power that Jesus gives. When Jesus calls you to a relationship with himself, he knows he is calling you to do something you can't do on your own. That's why he gives his forgiving and transforming grace. If your heart is cold toward Christ, ask him for forgiveness. Ask him for his power to change. Ask him to fill you with a burning desire to know him and to love him more than anything or anyone else. The Christ who calls you to relationship with him will be pleased with your dependence and will grant your request made in faith.

# Fighting for Purity with the Power of Grace

1. Are you guilty of pursuing Jesus only for what you can get from him? Ask for his help as you seek forgiveness and the power to change. Ask God to help you love Jesus for who he is, not merely for what he can do for you.

2. Find a passage in Scripture where you can meet with the Lord. Maybe it is John 6 or John 15. It might be Psalm 23 or Revelation 4. Whatever passage you select, pray the words of the text out loud.

3. Find a song with true lyrics that reflect the biblical gospel. The songs I mentioned in this chapter are "Amazing Grace," "It Is Well with My Soul," and "Before the Throne of God Above." These would be great places to start. Though it may seem strange, sing the songs out loud to the Lord. Don't worry if people are close by — sing under your breath and to the Lord. When it feels strange, pray for grace to quit thinking about yourself and to focus on the Lord.

4. Ask your accountability partner to join with you in these things.

# CONCLUSION

# A Call to Holiness and Hope

We have covered a lot of ground in this book. We have talked about how to use the grace of God in Jesus to put off pornography by putting on gratitude, humility, and accountability—just to name a few. These are all tangible ways to realize the grace of God in your life. I pray that as you have read this book, you have been experiencing these means of grace, and that you already see progress as you move toward freedom.

I want to conclude by beckoning you to holiness and purity as you continue your grace-filled journey toward freedom from pornography. I also want to point you to strong hope in Jesus as you wage the battle. I want to urge you toward these realities with two passages from 1 Thessalonians that I pray will motivate and energize you as you move from pornography to purity.

## A Call to Holiness

In 1 Thessalonians 4, the apostle Paul issues a strong call to live a holy life:

> It is God's will that you should be sanctified: that you should avoid sexual immorality; that each of you should learn to control your own body in a way that is holy and honorable, not in passionate lust like the pagans, who do not know God; and that in this matter no one should wrong or take advantage of a brother or sister. The Lord will punish all those who commit such sins, as we told you and warned you before. For God did not call us to be impure, but to live a holy life.
>
> *1 Thessalonians 4:3–7*

Paul begins his exhortation by describing the will of God in very practical terms. Many Christians ask complex questions about God's will. They search for it, agonize over it, and develop methods to discover it. Paul says he already knows what it is. The will of God is that Christians be "sanctified." By this, Paul means he wants Christians to be more like Christ. God's will, according to Paul, is for Christians to pursue the character of Christ as they grow in holiness.

As Paul describes the will of God as growing to be like Jesus, his very first instruction is that believers should avoid sexual immorality. In the mind of the apostle Paul, one of the main threats to being like Jesus is the temptation to indulge in immoral expressions of sexuality. Obviously the category of sexual immorality is larger than pornography, but pornography is one of the main ways in which people today engage in sexual sin. This means pornography is a significant threat to you! Pornography threatens your ability to live within

God's holy will because pornography is an obstacle to your growth in Jesus.

Paul continues to describe why sexual immorality is wrong. It displays a lack of self-control that characterizes the pagans who do not know God. This matches Paul's point when he urges the Ephesian believers, "So I tell you this, and insist on it in the Lord, that you must no longer live as the Gentiles do, in the futility of their thinking" (Ephesians 4:17). When Christians who have been immersed in the grace of Jesus look at pornography, they are engaging in the same graceless act as those who have rejected Jesus' infinite grace. Recipients of grace should act radically different than rejecters of grace.

Paul has already provided two powerful reasons to battle any form of sexual immorality. But he is not finished. He goes on to explain that sexual immorality is wrong because it hurts people. When you look at pornography, you "wrong or take advantage of a brother or sister." Pornography is opposed to growing more like Jesus because it harms others. Our goal as Christians is to be just like Jesus, who never walked around gazing at women and wondering how he could take physical advantage of them. This unchristian attitude is exactly what drives pornography. Pornography invites its consumers to think only about themselves and the selfish pleasures its actors can offer. When you look at pornography, you're not thinking about the damage you're doing to the actors you're watching or how you could love them and pray for them. When you look at pornography, you're not thinking about the damage you're doing to your spouse or children or other family members. You're not thinking about the pain you could inflict on those who love you in your church. You're not thinking about grieving the Holy Spirit. You're only thinking about yourself. Pornography is a wholly selfish act that eclipses the concerns, needs, and well-being of everyone around you. Therefore, Paul urges sexually immoral people toward holiness by urging them to consider, in a spirit of selflessness, how their sin deeply damages other people.

Paul ends his appeal where he began—with holiness. God "did not call us to be impure, but to live a holy life." The call to be in Christ is the call to be holy. Christian, hear the Word of God: the impurity of pornography stands in direct opposition to who you are in Christ. The blood of Jesus beckons you to holiness. You are summoned to look like Jesus. Therefore you must flee from living like an unbeliever and inflicting sexual harm on others. You must run passionately away from porn and toward holiness, love, self-control, and grace. The great call of your life is to be holy, as Jesus is holy. Pornography stands firmly opposed to that call. You must run from it and toward Christ.

## A Call to Hope

First Thessalonians 4 presents a strong call to holiness. Paul even makes clear that if you are not holy, the Lord will punish you. Those who persist in behaving like unbelievers and harming others through sexual immorality will be disciplined. The sternness of this warning on its own is a motivation to flee pornography and pursue holiness.

But we need to be careful. One of the main themes throughout this book is that we need the grace of Jesus in order to be like Jesus. Being holy and fleeing pornography require a power outside ourselves. This reality makes the next chapter in 1 Thessalonians vital. In 1 Thessalonians 5:23–24, Paul writes, "May God himself, the God of peace, sanctify you through and through. May your whole spirit, soul and body be kept blameless at the coming of our Lord Jesus Christ. The one who calls you is faithful, and he will do it."

I am persuaded that these two verses contain the most hopeful teaching in the Bible for Christians struggling with the sexual immorality of pornography. Here Paul provides a massive infusion of grace-filled hope enforcing the strong call to holiness given in 1 Thessalonians 4.

The command in 1 Thessalonians 4 is for Christians to avoid sexual immorality. The call is to quit harming others. The call is to be sanctified and holy. But undergirding those commands is this beautiful promise of grace in 1 Thessalonians 5. Here Paul teaches that as you pursue sanctification, *God himself*, the God of peace, will sanctify you. Paul bases the sanctification of God in your life on God's own inexhaustible faithfulness. Because God is perfectly good and perfectly powerful—because he is faithful—he will surely accomplish your sanctification. The key to Christlike holiness and freedom from pornography is to believe both 1 Thessalonians 4 and 5. We must fight for sanctification by avoiding the sexual immorality of pornography. We also, however, must not depend on our own resources, strategies, or willpower. Our resources will deteriorate, our strategies will fail, and our willpower will weaken. Rather, we need to put our trust in our faithful God, who will ultimately accomplish our sanctification by a demonstration of omnipotent grace.

## Matt's Journey toward Holiness and Hope

Do you remember Matt? I mentioned him in the very first line of the first chapter of this book. He was the college student who had been introduced to pornography by an uncle when he was a little boy. Though I've changed the names of the people mentioned in this book, I want you to know Matt's true identity. *I am Matt.*

I was introduced to pornography back in the day when people still watched VHS tapes. I was just an eight-year-old boy whose creepy uncle was completely enslaved to porn. He had videocassettes everywhere. One day he handed a tape to me and my friends. We watched it. To this day, I don't think I have ever seen anything quite so terrible and so wonderful. It was terrible because my guilty eight-year-old conscience screamed out that it was wrong. And it was wonderful, in a perverse way, because watching people commit these new and unimagined acts of immorality was exhilarating. The pornography I watched that afternoon opened up an intense struggle for me that lasted more than a decade.

By God's grace, I wasn't able to see very much pornography. There was no Internet when I was a kid. The only way to see pornography was to buy a magazine in the store (if you were old enough) or to be friends with someone who owned something. I was too young to buy it, and I wasn't around my perverted uncle very much. But the desire had been awakened. I wanted to see porn and would devour every rare glimpse I could catch. There was never a single occasion that I denied myself a peek at pornography when I had the opportunity.

When I was fourteen years old, I repented of my sins for the very first time and trusted in Christ alone for salvation.

I moved from knowing pornography was wrong to really hating it. But I still looked at it whenever I could because I simply didn't know what to do to be different. Over time, I began to struggle against my temptations, but I found myself consistently on the losing side of the battle. I just didn't know what to do. I would look at pornography whenever I could, and then spend days and weeks feeling guilty.

By the time I was in college, something had to give. My desires to see pornography whenever I could were in a raging conflict with my increasing desire to be in a close relationship with Jesus. Over time, I began to do many of the things described in this book. I began to draw near to Jesus in repentant prayer, asking for his forgiving and changing grace; I took radical measures to eliminate any potential opportunity I had to view pornography; I sought wise accountability; and I began to serve others. As I began taking these steps, I witnessed a miracle in my life. I began to change. I noticed a definite decrease in my desire for porn and an increasing desire for Jesus. The change wasn't instantaneous; it rarely is. But it was *real* change.

The first sign of this change was when I began to talk honestly with the Lord about my sin and to seek his grace for forgiveness and change. A second indication appeared as I began to talk honestly with brothers in Christ about my struggle. After that, I continued to see change as I began to choose purity over pornography in moments of temptation. My record wasn't perfect, but no longer was it defined by constant, habitual failure.

The major milestone of victory over this temptation occurred when I was twenty-two. I had graduated from college and was driving the thousand miles between Southern Seminary in Kentucky (where I had begun my seminary education) and Gordon College in Massachusetts (where my future wife, Lauren, was finishing up her college degree). I was driving in the middle of the night when I passed the largest pornographic video store on planet Earth. As the store came into view, I had two opposing thoughts. The first was that in this moment I had the best opportunity to look at pornography that anyone could ever want. It was the middle of the night. I was in the middle of nowhere. And nobody I knew was around. I could stop and look at pornography for hours, and there would be no consequences. This was the sort of opportunity I would have dreamed of having just a few short years ago.

But even as I considered this opportunity, there was a second, more powerful thought—I didn't *want* to stop. I really didn't want to see pornography. I had no interest in what they were selling in that store. Over the years of fighting, prayer, and accountability, God had been faithful and had truly changed my desires. Though I could have looked at all the porn I wanted to, I didn't desire it any longer. I was free.

Being free does not mean being perfect. Over the years since that day, I have still needed to walk closely with the Lord, engage the fight early, repent from an impure heart, and be accountable to other men. I am not yet what I will be. But by God's grace, I am not what I was. I write these words to you today as a man who does not look at pornography—and does not desire to. The reason is not that I am so wonderful, but that I have experienced the same grace of Christ I'm commending in this book.

I want you to know my story because I want you to be persuaded that the powerful grace I'm writing about is more than words on a page. The Bible is a living and active sword

(Hebrews 4:12). Its message of grace is a powerful and vibrant message that God used to transform me. He will use it to transform you.

I don't know if your struggle with pornography is more or less extreme than mine was. But it doesn't matter. Whatever you perceive the degree of your struggle to be—whether minor or major—your sin is enough for a just and vengeful God to send you to hell forever. As true as that statement is, whether your struggle is major or minor, your sin is not nearly as strong as the grace of Jesus to transform you.

*"Where sin increased, grace increased all the more"* (Romans 5:20).

If you are trusting in Jesus, pornography will never have the final say in your life. Forty-five zillion years from now, pornography will be nowhere in your mind as you perpetually behold the beauty of the spotless Lamb who was slain for your sin and mine. There is a day coming—and it is not far away—when you will see Jesus himself. When you see him, he will change you into his perfect likeness.

The message of this book is that you do not have to wait until then to be free of pornography. The journey away from pornography can begin today as you walk the grace-filled path charted in these pages. Fellow child of God, I write these words with one final prayer—that you might know the hope that, in Christ, you can be finally free from pornography. The grace of Jesus guarantees it.

# Help for Families and Friends of Men Struggling with Pornography

Many lives are touched when pornography is uncovered in a man's life. Wives feel the pain and betrayal most acutely, so I want to speak to them primarily. I also want to help if you are the fiancée, daughter, son, mother, father, friend, or fellow church member of a man who is struggling. I want you to see that Scripture speaks to your pain in straightforward and practical ways.

Discovering that a loved one is struggling with pornography is always painful. You have likely experienced an explosion of emotions, including betrayal, anger, sorrow, disgust, fear, and compassion, along with deep worry that your relationship may never be restored. In this book I have labored to point men to the grace of Christ that is available to them in their struggle to be forgiven and changed. Here I want to share with you a particular grace of Jesus that is available as you respond to the sin of someone else as it deeply affects you.

As you read, I want you to understand that I have helped many people in your position. I have seen the pain and devastation that floods out of the lives of those men who indulge in pornography. You very likely feel overwhelmed, enraged, and profoundly troubled by what your loved one has been doing behind your back. You may be feeling like you are alone in your experience of shock and pain. If you do, I want to encourage you that you are not alone. Consider the strong words of the author of Hebrews:

> Therefore, since we have a great high priest who has ascended into heaven, Jesus the Son of God, let us hold firmly to the faith we profess. For we do not have a high priest who is unable to empathize with our weaknesses, but we have one who has been tempted in every way, just as we are—yet he did not sin. Let us then approach God's throne of grace with confidence, so that we may receive mercy and find grace to help us in our time of need.
>
> *Hebrews 4:14–16*

This passage explodes with relevance for you. At least three helpful truths are presented here to minister to you in your pain.

First, these verses promise that mercy and grace are available to you in your time of need. When despair overwhelms you and fury overtakes you, it can be tempting, in the flood of emotion, to believe that no help is available. You need to believe the promise of God that his mercy and grace are available to you. God loves you and will help you.

Second, Jesus sympathizes with you in your weaknesses

and temptations and shows you how to respond without sinning. Jesus was betrayed by a man who was very close to him. He knows what it's like to be in relationship with a person whose behavior behind one's back is the opposite of what it is to one's face. Jesus responded to these trials without sinning. Jesus is our example who shows us it is possible, with his help, to respond to suffering in ways that are righteous and loving.

Third, you receive mercy and grace from Jesus himself when you draw near to him. The author of Hebrews promises that we find mercy and grace to help when we approach God's throne of grace. You will know the overflowing care and comfort of Christ when you draw near to him in prayer. Oh, how I pray for you to do this as I write these words! When you feel frustrated, sorrowful, angry, and betrayed, don't let those distressing thoughts merely run through your head. Instead, direct them to God. When you experience these strong emotions, remember to talk to the Lord about them. Approach the throne of grace and tell God how you feel. Ask him for this promised help to know how to respond. Plead with him to care for you in the midst of this extreme difficulty. When you draw near to him in faith, he will never turn you away but will help you as he provides you his grace and mercy. If you have never prayed about this situation, then stop reading right now and talk to Jesus about your emotions, ask him for his grace to help, and believe that he will give it to you.

Praying in this way is something you must continue to do over the long haul as you walk with your loved one on his path toward change. I want to point you to practical steps you need to take as you seek to act with wisdom as you recover from the pain you are experiencing. First, however, I want to tell you a story that can help answer a question you may have.

## Men and Pornography

Stephanie didn't believe a word Chad said. After several years of marriage, Stephanie discovered that Chad was secretly indulging in pornography. She woke up one night and discovered him at the computer in his home office. As she quietly approached from behind, she was completely horror-struck by the images playing on the screen. In the days that followed, Stephanie shed tears of anger and sorrow as Chad responded to her questions with answers she wanted but hated hearing. Chad's answers to one of her questions left her in a state of total disbelief.

Stephanie was convinced that Chad must believe she was ugly or he wouldn't be looking at other women for sexual satisfaction. Stephanie was concerned about baby weight she was carrying and was sure this was the reason Chad had turned to pornography. Chad insisted, "Stephanie, I think you're beautiful. This has nothing to do with you." Stephanie found this impossible to believe.

Stephanie's disbelief was understandable because Chad's answer was a half-truth. On the one hand, Chad said his sin had nothing to do with Stephanie. He meant that he loved his wife and thought she was pretty, but it was going too far to say that his sin had *nothing* to do with her. Chad had compromised his marriage vows, betrayed Stephanie's trust, and brought severe damage into their life. His sin had everything to do with Stephanie, and he needed to learn to quit saying such things.

On the other hand, Chad sincerely believed his wife was attractive. Stephanie needed a lot of help understanding how Chad could sincerely think that and still look at pornography. If you're in the same situation as Stephanie, perhaps you have a similar concern. Your husband's struggle may have made you self-conscious about your physical appearance, and you may believe that if you were more attractive, your husband wouldn't have looked at pornography.

If this is your concern, then you need to know that your husband's problem with pornography has nothing to do with your appearance—no matter what you look like or what you *think* you look like. You can lose weight, gain weight, change your hair and make-up, or undergo plastic surgery, and it would not fix his problem. Nothing you do to your appearance will solve the problem because pornography is your husband's sin, not yours. Two realities demonstrate this truth.

First, God commands men to be satisfied with the physical appearance of their wives (Proverbs 5:19). God gives no ideal body weight, eye color, height, or hairstyle that is to be desired. He commands men to desire their wives. Whatever you look like should be your husband's ideal. *Your* physical appearance is what he is called to desire. If there's a breakdown here, it's his failure to desire what God calls him to desire, not your failure to look a certain way.

The second issue has to do with the logic of lust. Lust, by definition, wants what it does not have. Lust always looks past what it possesses to the object it lacks. This is why Chad's statement about his wife is quite true in a sense. Chad's lust for pornography is not about Stephanie's looks; it is about wanting a woman he doesn't have, regardless of

Stephanie's appearance. Stephanie could change her entire appearance and it wouldn't fix her husband's lust. Chad needs Jesus to cure his lust by giving him a heart full of grateful contentment rather than a heart that desires a woman who is not his wife.

## Walking the Path to Restoration

The bottom line is that pornography is your husband's sin. It is not yours. As you walk the difficult path to restoration with your husband, you must avoid making your appearance responsible for your husband's sin. Here are five practical things you can do as you seek to help your husband and move forward in a growing, vibrant, and happy marriage.

### 1. Don't Struggle Alone — Get Help

In addition to calling out to the Lord for his mercy and grace in time of need, you must seek the aid of wise Christians. Your situation will be filled with dozens of particulars that need specific wisdom beyond the generalities of any book. You will need others to help sort through them. The idea of reaching out to others for help may make you nervous. You may think you can handle this alone, or you may feel too embarrassed to tell a pastor or close female friend. I urge you to think about this a bit more.

The Bible encourages us to live our lives together with other Christians. The apostle Paul writes, "Encourage one another and build each other up, just as in fact you are doing" (1 Thessalonians 5:11). The writer of Hebrews states, "Let us consider how we may spur one another on toward love and good deeds, not giving up meeting together, as some are in the habit of doing, but encouraging one another—and all the more as you see the Day approaching" (Hebrews 10:24–25). Christians need other Christians for mutual encouragement and for support in becoming people who are devoted to love and good deeds.

As you move toward reconciliation, there will be times when you are discouraged, angry, and drawn toward being unkind. You need people in the fight who will spur you toward right responses. One of the most important things you can do after you talk to God is to talk to a pastor or close female friend. Ask for their wisdom and prayers. Make sure someone is available who will reach out to you and will let you reach out to them when you're struggling.

## 2. Deal with Your Emotions Biblically

If you're like most people, you've been overwhelmed by a flood of emotion in the aftermath of your discovery. The emotions you're experiencing are most likely some kind of anger or sadness. When you think of the betrayal you have experienced and the shock you have endured, you may even be dismayed by the depth of these feelings. There is a ton to say about understanding and dealing with these emotions from a biblical perspective, but I'll mention two points for now.

If you are angry and sad that your husband viewed pornography, your feelings are appropriate. It may surprise you to hear this from me, but it is true. God's response to sin is not neutral, and yours shouldn't be either. God gets angry and sad over sin (see Hebrews 3:17). When we share these emotions, we show that our affections are in line with God's. In fact, it would be a mark of wickedness for you to respond to sin with neutrality or happiness. In the midst of such a difficult situation, it is important that you understand the legitimacy of the strong emotions you're experiencing, lest you place undue guilt on yourself for your appropriate response to the sin of your loved one.

There's more to say about this issue, however. It is legitimate to be angry and sad over sin, but this reality does not give you a blank check to respond any way you want. Though God responds to wickedness with anger and sorrow, he never sins. Your emotions will be like God's when your anger and sorrow toward your husband are free from sin (see Ephesians 4:26). Two principles can help ensure that your anger and sadness are righteous, thereby avoiding sin.

First, your anger and sorrow are sinful when they are unrestrained, so you must fight for self-control when you experience these emotions. If you've responded to your husband with screaming fits, cussing rants, spiteful threats to expose him to those he respects, physical violence of any kind, or intimations that you will keep him from his children, then you are sinning in your response to your husband. If you have been guilty of such reactions, you need to pursue the forgiving and transforming grace of Christ. If you know Christ, you are not a slave to your emotions. Christ himself can give you the grace to have righteous anger and virtuous sorrow when you ask him for these things in faith.

Second, your anger and sorrow are sinful when they keep you from being restored to your husband. Though God is angry and sad over sin, he seeks resolution. God moves to deal with his displeasure over sin through the atoning work of Jesus Christ. In a similar way, your strong emotions should lead you toward reconciliation and restoration rather than away from it. If your reaction has led you to avoid your husband for a prolonged period of time, then you need to begin to pursue the forgiving and transforming grace of Christ. You may feel as though restoration is a million miles away, but Jesus has power to get you there when you believe in him. It's essential that you fight for restoration in your relationship with your husband.

## 3. Fight to Forgive

The call to move toward reconciliation leads to a critical step that you must take. Ultimately, you must forgive your husband for his sin. The apostle Paul writes, "Be kind and compassionate to one another, forgiving each other, just as in Christ God forgave you" (Ephesians 4:32). For those who have been sinned against in dramatic fashion, this passage can seem like one of the most controversial in the Bible. The call on your life to forgive may seem overwhelming—even impossible. How can you forgive in the face of such pain? How can you pardon in the midst of such betrayal? You must forgive the way you have been forgiven in Christ. The Bible grounds the command to forgive in the forgiveness we have received from Christ.

We are to forgive others precisely because God has forgiven us. Sometimes it's possible to believe that a refusal to forgive is a statement about the seriousness of the sin committed against you and is a holy intolerance of it. Though this can *seem* true, it really isn't. Ephesians 4:32 teaches that no matter how terribly you have been sinned against, an ultimate failure to forgive is a failure to consider how much you have been forgiven. Show me someone who refuses to forgive others, and I'll show you someone arrogantly refusing to consider the number of sins for which God has forgiven them.

For many of you, the problem is not that you don't want to forgive, but that you don't know how to forgive. Paul is helpful in dealing with this issue as well. He tells us we are to forgive the way we have been forgiven in Christ. Jeremiah 31:34 describes how we've been forgiven. In the context of this passage, the prophet Jeremiah is anticipating the work that Jesus will come to do. In unpacking this work, Jeremiah mentions an amazing benefit of the coming of the Messiah, quoting God himself as declaring that in Christ he will no longer remember our sins: "I will forgive their wickedness and will remember their sins no more."

It is critical to understand what this does not mean. God does not mean he forgets about our sin as though he develops some sort of divine amnesia. God has perfect knowledge of all things—past, present, and future. He knows the end from the beginning. When God says he doesn't remember our sins, he's not limiting his perfect knowledge. Instead he means he doesn't remember our sins *against us*. God knows we sinned, but he does not allow that sin to impact his relationship with us.

Your forgiveness of your husband will be like God's forgiveness of you when you extend grace to him and have a relationship with him that does not hold his sin against him. As your husband is fighting for grace-empowered change, you need to commit to moving toward a restored relationship in every area of your marriage. This restoration will not be immediate. The important thing at first is to be committed to getting there. After that, you need to work closely with the person helping you to plan a wise path forward with your husband as a married couple walking in forgiveness.

## 4. Confess Your Sins

Your husband is responsible for his sin of looking at pornography. You are not to blame for your husband's sexual immorality. There is nothing you can do and nothing in the way you look that can force your husband to sin sexually since immorality comes from within his heart and not because of outward circumstances. It's really important for you to know, however, that this is a sword that cuts both ways. You are not to blame for your husband's sin, but neither is he responsible for yours.

In the aftermath of the disclosure of a serious sin like pornography, many women focus almost entirely on their husband's sin and forget that they are sinners too. You must work against this tendency by humbly considering your own sin, and not just your husband's. Have you responded with sinful emotions to your husband's sin? Have you failed to forgive him? Did you fail to have an active sexual relationship with him before you knew about his problem? There is no expectation of immediate sexual restoration after you discovered his sin, but have you been guilty of withholding sexual affection for a prolonged period of time after he has sought forgiveness? You will never be at fault for your husband's sin, but it is possible that you need to seek forgiveness for your own sin in these and other areas.

## 5. Be a Wife, Not a Cop

Chad and Stephanie began to take the journey toward restoration as a couple. Chad was repenting of his unthankful heart and growing in gratitude for Stephanie and in his integrity with God, his wife, and other people. His progress was not without problems, but he was changing. Stephanie was learning to forgive Chad for his failures and to seek forgiveness for her own sins. As they grew together, Stephanie was having a tough time trusting Chad. After the years of being in the dark regarding such a serious sin, Stephanie was determined not to get burned again. She became vigilant, always looking over Chad's shoulder. She insisted on receiving the reports from his accountability software, constantly checked the browser history on his phone, and asked skeptical questions about women at his work. On one occasion she was unjustly suspicious that he was looking at pornography at work and insisted that he take a lie detector test to disprove her doubts.

Most people understand Stephanie's struggle to trust her husband after his sinful abuse of confidence, but her response was doing more damage to their marriage. She never intended to make things more difficult. She was trying to deal with the problem in the only way she knew how. In spite of this motivation, there were two main problems with Stephanie's response.

First, Stephanie's efforts will never lead to a more trusting relationship with her husband. Stephanie's constant investigations of Chad weren't helping her learn to trust her husband; rather, they were helping her learn to trust in her ability to keep tabs on him. If you only believe your husband after seeing accountability reports and the results of lie detector tests, then you're not trusting your husband. Instead, you're trusting the reports and results.

Second, Stephanie was focusing on the wrong job. Chad did need accountability. He needed software that blocked porn on his computer. He needed a wise Christian mentor to ask him hard questions about his actions and desires. He needed all of these things and more, but she couldn't be the one to give them.

So it is for you too. You need to focus on being your husband's wife, not a cop enforcing purity in his life. You need to know and trust the person who is helping him, and you need to be confident about the accountability measures that are in place in his life. You need to be aware that he is seriously pursuing Christ, and you need to have access to speak with him and the person helping him when you have concerns. If you try to lead the accountability effort in his life, however, I promise it will have a corrosive effect on your marriage. Focus on being married to your husband. Pray for grace to draw near to him and pursue closeness relationally, spiritually, physically, and in every other way. Allow others to focus on enforcement.

In the early days, try running questions and concerns by the person helping you before you go to your husband with them. This person can help you evaluate how pressing your concerns are and whether they're wise. For example, many women want specific details about the pornography their husbands were viewing. These kinds of details aren't good to know. Though you may think it will be helpful, knowing them will only make reconciliation harder than it already is. Seek out wisdom from others on this and other matters.

## Moving Forward with Mercy and Grace

As you move toward restoration there will be many steps on the journey. Don't forget that Jesus gives you his mercy and grace in your time of need as you draw near to him. Jesus loves you, and he will help you. Women sometimes struggle because they focus on their husband and wrongly believe that what they need above everything else is a husband who does not look at pornography. It is certainly a wonderful blessing to have a husband who doesn't look at porn, but that is not the most important thing in your marriage. What you ultimately need more than anything else is the mercy and grace that come from Jesus. Jesus' mercy and grace is yours by trusting in him—whether or not you have a husband who looks at porn.

When you have, by faith, this mercy and grace, you will be empowered to reach out for help, to respond with righteous emotions, to move toward your husband in forgiveness, to deal with your own sin, and to trust, not only your husband, but, more importantly, the Lord, who promises that his goodness and mercy will follow you all the days of your life. This promise is true, and it is yours, regardless of whether or not your husband ever looks at pornography again. Because Jesus has made this promise to you, you can be set free by his mercy and grace to love your husband in spite of his sin. When you do this, you will be loving your husband in the same way Jesus loves you.

# Acknowledgments

This book has been in the works for years. From the beginning of my pastoral ministry, I've been counseling young men who have been caught in the struggle with pornography. I've been preaching on this topic in churches, lecturing on it in classes, and teaching about it at conferences. What I have written here has been simmering for years in the cauldron of church ministry.

The process of writing down my thoughts has been an effort I have not undertaken alone. I have several people to thank.

I am grateful to Al Mohler, Russell Moore, and Dan DeWitt. I serve under these godly men at Southern Seminary and Boyce College and am thankful for their Christian conviction, faithful leadership, and encouragement to pursue writing projects like this one.

I am also thankful for the elders at Crossing Church where I have been privileged to serve as the pastor of biblical living. These gracious, wise, and humble men are faithful colaborers in the kingdom of Christ. It has been a great encouragement to count on their prayers throughout this project.

I must express appreciation for the team at Zondervan. I am so thankful for their support of this project and for the shared commitment to making this book be as good as it can possibly be. Ryan Pazdur, in particular, has become a trusted adviser and faithful friend for whom I am profoundly grateful.

Three people provided helpful comments as I was writing. My research assistant Sean Perron, my assistant Amber Walsh, and fellow pastor Dave Northrup all shared valuable insights that improved the quality and clarity of my work here.

Gunner Gundersen served as my editorial assistant on this book. Gunner is a faithful servant of Christ, and he was invaluable to me on this project. He pored over each chapter and made meticulous edits. Even when I didn't adopt his recommendations, he always helped me see my writing from a fresh vantage point and greatly improved this book.

I also must express how grateful I am for my wife, Lauren, and my three children, Carson, Chloe, and Connor. Lauren is the most supportive wife in the world. She has prayed for me, encouraged me, provided feedback, and taken care of me during the writing process. My children were also an encouragement. Almost every day they would ask about "Daddy's book" and tell me they were praying for me. The great honor of my life is to come home every day to my four favorite people in the world.

Finally, I must give praise and glory to God. While writing this book, I have truly experienced the kindness of God in his provision for me. Working on each chapter has reminded me of the amazing God we serve, who is abounding in grace. My prayer is that you encounter his grace in the pages of this book.

*Heath Lambert, Louisville, Kentucky*
*July 2012*